THE TORMENT OF SECRECY

The Background and Consequences of American Security Policies

EDWARD A. SHILS

The Torment of Secrecy

THE BACKGROUND AND CONSEQUENCES
OF AMERICAN SECURITY POLICIES

THE FREE PRESS, GLENCOE, ILLINOIS

To

ROBERT HUTCHINS

and

MICHAEL POLANYI

ACKNOWLEDGMENTS

I am grateful to the Fund for the Republic, and the Committee on Social Thought of the University of Chicago for facilitating my work on this book.

—THE AUTHOR

Contents

7

Foreword

AFTER NEARLY A DECADE of degrading agitation and numerous unnecessary and unworthy actions, the disturbance aroused in the United States by the preoccupation with secrecy and subversion has begun to abate. All is not yet entirely serene. Many of the injustices committed have not yet been righted—if they can ever be righted—and security policies are not yet sufficiently realistic, but the abatement is substantial and genuine.

This abatement should provide no occasion for self-congratulation. This is not the moment to praise the fundamental common sense of most of our citizenry, or the deeper strength of our institutions, or our capacity to resist, when the decisive time comes, the seductions of demagogues. It is not to be gainsaid that all of these virtues have played their fitting part, nor are they to be denied their due praise for having saved us from further disgrace. A great society should not allow its partial recovery from a humiliating and unjustifiable lapse from decent conduct to diminish the necessity for the conscientious scrutiny of that lapse. It must try to understand in the most detached and unimpassioned way what that lapse signifies in terms of its own history and general principles. It must reaffirm and clarify its standards and turn a cold eye on its weaknesses.

The Torment of Secrecy is presented as an exploratory effort to meet these obligations. It was first written, in the heat of the struggle, as a broadside against the depredations of Senators McCarthy and McCarran and the unwholesome forces which they had let loose by their example and encouragement. It became clear, however, in the course of

9

further consideration, that it would be more useful to interpret the significance of the noxious happenings of the past ten years in the light of the tasks and traditions of American life and the principles of the free society, than to review once more and in detail the crudities and enormities of our security and loyalty policies, and to condemn them in the strongest terms. I have not foreborne to condemn, either explicitly or implicitly, but I have tried to mold the book into something more than a polemic. I have tried to show how our recent inconveniences have arisen from the encounter of certain of our less gratifying traditions with certain events of the real world and how, as a result of these traditions, we have distorted and exaggerated a genuine problem and overloaded it with features drawn from the world of traditional phantasies and passions. In order to arrive at a more fundamental appreciation of the quest for security, I have thought it appropriate to analyze in a more general way, some features of the role of secrecy in modern society and its interplay with privacy and publicity which are so intimately connected with it. Similarly, I have thought it desirable after having shown a vital connection between extremism and an obsession with the security and insecurity of secrecy, to assert in more general terms the principles which characterize pluralism and which condemn extremism. Thus, through the analysis of the destructive potentialities of certain traditions in confrontation with the real problem of security, what began as a polemic became a reformulation of the principles of a free, lasting and dignified society. *The Torment of Secrecy* is an essay in sociological analysis and political philosophy which, having taken its origin in a concrete problem of contemporary American life, aspires to provide some guiding lines for the improvement of the situation which called it forth.

I

With regard to the improvement of our security policy in the next years, the first thing to be said is that our policy has not been realistic. The reporting in Geneva this past

August of approximately identical results obtained by scientists working on the same problem and in the same intellectual tradition but without communication, has demonstrated very forcibly what was already well known before. Our policies were inadequate to preserve our secrets.

Intended in the first place to prevent the Soviet Union from acquiring scientific and technological information connected with national defense, events have shown that the rigor and comprehensiveness of our security measures have not been successful in preventing Soviet and other scientists from gaining our knowledge through their own scientific exertions. In science, the true bearer of secrets is Nature, and no security policy can prohibit it from disclosing these secrets from others who are qualified to interrogate it.

In addition to being concerned with secrets which could not be kept, our security policy has been concerned with secrets which need not be kept. Superfluous as well as insoluble tasks have been given to our security services. The real and difficult task of security policy is to prevent the disclosure of a very limited range of information which ought to be kept secret, and to prevent the entry into posts of central relevance to national security and internal order, of persons with subversive intentions or propensities.

These legitimate tasks of security policy are unlikely to disappear as long as the possibility of war and the need for military defense remain. It is unlikely that these dangers and the needs to which they give rise can be dissipated to any great extent, failing the establishment of a rigorous and comprehensive system of the international control of nuclear weapons and a great change in the system of international relations.

Thus, even if the problem were reduced to its essential dimensions, the maintenance of an effective security system would continue to be a pressing affair. Even if security officers become wiser and less prejudiced than they often are, and even if American politicians become more restrained and circumspect, and all become more perceptive of the costs as well the limitations of any security policy, the safeguarding of secrecy will still be difficult and it will still be necessary.

In that event, we shall have with us for a considerable time to come an irritant to the public peace. As long as the dangers of espionage exist, i.e., as long as we have some knowledge which a potential enemy desires, which can do us harm when it is in his possession and which he cannot obtain except by espionage, we will have a genuine security problem. As long as the genuine security problem exists, there will be persons whose imagination will be set boiling with excited apprehension. The mere existence of secrecy is bound to set nervous minds on edge. It has been the extension of the influence of these nervous minds which has caused so much trouble in the past decade. It was our readiness to admit to positions of influence persons nervously obsessed with loyalty and disloyalty, with secrecy and publicity which compounded many times over the technical difficulties of an efficient security policy.

Hence the improvement of our security policy depends not only on technical and administrative improvements and on better training for the personnel of security. It depends also on the improvement of the environment in which the necessary policy of security is conducted. The chances of the reduction to a minimum of the sound and fury aroused by the task of protecting the necessary minimum of secrecy, depend on the subsidence of one tradition of American life and the isolation of another.

II

The discussion of secrecy and subversion has been a continuation of deeper and older traditions which have been obscured by the terms in which its most recent phase has been conducted. The enraged demand for a rigid security policy as broad as public life itself, the anxious and evasive denial that there is any need for any security policy at all, and even the reasonable and realistic argument put forward among scientists in favor of a security policy which would eschew the slovenly determination of untrustworthiness through long-past activities and associations and which would be confined to strictly military projects—all of these arguments are intertwined with other arguments which are carried on passions which do not acknowledge their own existence. The conflict which has disgraced American society has not been just a conflict as to whether certain scientific, technical and administrative knowledge should be kept secret or whether it was inimical to national security to allow persons who had once been Communists, fellow-travellers, or their friends, to be employed in the film industry, in advertising agencies, in wireless and television broadcasting, or in the Federal or State Civil Services. In fact, it would be nearer the truth to say that for most of the participants, the protection of secrecy and the prevention of subversion have only been pretexts for the continuation of a conflict begun much earlier and quite without relation to the problems of security.

III

The agitation of the past decade about secrecy and subversion has been only a new turn in the conflict which has been going on in the United States with fluctuating severity and in various forms since the second quarter of the nineteenth century. It has been only the flaring up on another front of the long war between, on the one side, intellectuals and, on the other, politicians and businessmen, driven and dragged forward by small bands of phantasy-obsessed extremists spread thinly over many strata and professions.

It is in the attenuation of this traditional conflict that the prospect of an improvement of our situation rests. There are grounds for moderate optimism. For twenty-five years, the century-old estrangement between politicians and intellectuals has been declining. The acerbity and the injustices of the latest phase have, in fact, been by-products of an improvement on both sides. The hostility against the "Brain Trust" was only the friction accompanying the general acceptance of the entry of the intellectuals into politics and administration. The discreditable efflorescence of Com-

munism and fellow-travelling among the intellectuals in the
1930's and 1940's, was the less estimable but understandable
side of the fumbling and naive acceptance of civil responsibilities on the part of the intellectuals. It was a faltering
detour by persons who had been misguided by the anti-
political tradition which had prevailed among American
intellectuals for over a century.

It was a misjudgment arising from naiveté, vanity and
an ill-conceived sense of public responsibility and moral
concern. It was meanly exploited—first by the Communists
in the 1930's and 1940's and then in the 1940's and 1950's
by the nativist extremists, those mirror-images of the Communists. Senators McCarthy, McCarran and Jenner, Representatives Dies, Velde, Thomas, and about two dozen other
Congressmen—by their crudity and vindictiveness—Mr. Hiss,
Mr. Chambers, Prof. Lattimore, Miss Bentley, Mr. Budenz
and several score more—by their malicious espionage or
their frivolous and thoughtless fellow-travelling—have co-
operated in delaying the expiration of the tradition of
estrangement. The handful of the politicians, extremist or
unscrupulous, who are the carriers of the old tradition have
bolstered the long-standing prejudices of many intellectuals
just as the small number of civilly blind and morally frivolous
intellectuals have reanimated the distrustful prejudices of
the politicians. Yet, in both professions—among both intellectuals and politicians—closer collaboration and the cultivation of a sense of affinity has been going on now for a
considerable period of years.

McCarthyism has slowed down and harmed the process
of reconciliation between politicians and intellectuals. Nonetheless, it appears that the death of this obnoxious tradition
is a certainty of the second half of this century. McCarthyism and the continuing activities of the Un-American Activities Committee must be seen as a dying fire, momentarily
revived to a high blaze by a strong wind, as a futile rearguard struggle of the proponents of a tradition in the course
of its extinction, as a last desperate action of the diehards
who refuse to give up the beliefs and prerogatives of pop-

ulistic politicians in their relations with intellectuals as
scientists, scholars and administrators.

IV

Even if this tradition is helped to its grave by fore-
bearance and tact, and the acknowledgment of mutual obligations on the part of both intellectuals and politicians,
there will remain another tradition which has been at least
equally injurious. This is the nativist tradition—the tradition
of rancorous intolerance, of parochial jealousy, of intellectual
inferiority, of the dislike of foreigners, of the distrust of
urbanity, of the paranoid fear of subversion. Like the flirta-
tion with revolutionary ideas, it is not to be expected that
this frame of mind will in the foreseeable future disappear
entirely from the United States. It is one of our traditions,
and the nature of the personalities who carry it on from
generation to generation renders it unlikely that it will die
away out of their realistic recognition of the falsity of their
beliefs and the irrelevance of their sentiments. This tradition
need not, however, always be as harmful as it has been in
recent years in the United States. There is no reason why it
cannot be confined to the alleys and bars and back streets
and to the hate-filled hearts of the miserable creatures who
espouse it. This can be done if the inclinations, sometimes
faint and sometimes clear, of some of our politicians towards
this tradition are kept from becoming solid convictions, and
if those who have within themselves such dispositions become aware of the dangers of intimate connections with
those in whom the tradition is more full-blown. In other
words, since lunacy cannot be entirely eliminated, those
who share responsibility for conducting our affairs must not
form alliances with it.

It is from these alliances that the damage has come. In
the recent history of these alliances, the intellectuals themselves bear a special responsibility. For no intellectually
legitimate reason, they allow themselves to be drawn into
an alliance with Communist extremism. This alliance, although frivolous, had few directly damaging consequences.

Indirectly, however, it had the ugly consequence of generating the alliance of conservative politicians and businessmen with a band of moral desperadoes. This alliance produced one of the most unpleasant disorders in our history.

This instructs us. The lesson is that those who traffic with extremism become its victims. Just as the intellectuals of the 1930's and 1940's became the dupes of the Communist Party, so the politicians of the 1940's and 1950's who heeded the bellowing of their more mad constituents or who allowed themselves to be drawn into the circle of Senator McCarthy's whirlpool, found themselves deprived of their reason and their autonomy.

V

In the course of its history, America has on the whole avoided the great turbulences issuing from ideological politics. For the past two decades it has been rather less successful in preventing the intrusion into the domain of serious politics of the fanaticism which is associated with ideology. In the last few years the grip of ideological politics has become looser. The ideology of the "left" has passed into dissolution and the ideology of the "right," never elaborately articulated, has retracted into the lairs of its usual custodians.

The passing of passions of ideological politics should, however, be followed by the evaporation of the mythology of "left" and "right" as the two poles of political life at which reside the sacred and the diabolical.

If American society is to find the balance of publicity, privacy and secrecy which will maintain liberties, it must avoid the temptation to honor those who live at the poles of enthusiasm for the sacred and hatred for the diabolical. The fulfillment of perfection, of completeness, of total security is not for man here below. This does not mean that all should not be made as good as it can be; it means only that those who believe in the complete and perfect realization of any value had better be avoided by men who cherish the order of their lives and the decency of their society.

The perfectionists of security and loyalty, like the per-

fectionists of justice and freedom are a menace to freedom,
to justice and security and to the order to which loyalty is
demanded. A few perfectionists here and there in society
are vital to our well-being: a movement of perfectionists of
any sort is dangerous. Although idealism is as necessary to
the good society as moderation and complacency, an excess
can do great damage.

There are times for heroism and for tilting at windmills
and there are times when completeness and perfection must
be striven for in order to achieve no more than modest results. They must always be countered by matter-of-factness,
the acceptance of the intractability of the world and the
obstinacy of the old Adam within us, if vain disorders are
to be avoided. Political genius consists in sensing the moment when heroism and the quest for perfection are called
for; political madness consists in demanding them at all
times.

In this sense the argument put forward in this book
might be called conservative. The scribes of the conventicles,
staggering back from Marxism might even claim to find in
it some of the "New Conservatism." If they do, they will
be knocking at the wrong door. There is no yearning here
for any "good old days" before the Fall and there are no
expectations of salvation. A matter-of-fact humanitarian
socialism is just as compatible with the viewpoint expressed
in this book as a lively system of capitalist private enterprise, an undoctrinaire disposition towards equality can be
as much at home here as desire to maintain distinctions of
status, even vulgarity and good taste, the hero and the
philistine, could equally find a resting place in our argument for pluralistic moderation presented here. What is imperative, however, is more reasonableness and common
sense, more of a sense of affinity throughout our public life,
less eagerness to magnify differences and to seek false allies
at the extremes.

This demand is not utopian. It calls for something already in existence as a deeply rooted tradition of our national
life. If it had not existed, the tensions of the past decade

would have done us a measure of harm more commensurate with the enraged tempers and febrile enthusiasms of the main antagonists in the struggle for perfect security and maximal loyalty. What is needed is a more active appreciation of this beneficent tradition and a more conscientious refusal of the twin enthusiasms of alienated traditionalism and alienated radicalism.

EDWARD A. SHILS

PART I

Secrecy: Restriction and Overflow

CHAPTER 1

PUBLICITY, PRIVACY AND SECRECY:

THEIR EQUILIBRIUM AND

ITS DISRUPTION

I. *The Public and the Private*

A FREE SOCIETY can exist only when public spirit is balanced by an equal inclination of men to mind their own business. A society without a lively responsiveness to the facts of public life and without a concern for the shape of the community would collapse into a swamp of apathy, ruled by oligarchy. But, a society where men were interested only in what is remote from their own doorsteps would be a bedlam of overheated passions. No society is capable of sustaining the unremitting interest of all its citizens all the time, or even of most of its citizens most of the time, in the problems of the larger society.

The equal and continuous love of one's own and other men's liberties is as little to be expected as the preference for the good of the more inclusive community. Both the love of public liberty and the preference for the common good dominate the action of only a minority, even with most free societies, and it is not necessary that it be otherwise. This being so, however, it is important that the public sphere not be overcrowded.

Democracy requires the occasional political participation of most of its citizenry some of the time, and a moderate and dim perceptiveness—as if from the corner of the eye—the rest of the time. It could not function if politics and the state of the social order were always on everyone's mind. If most men, most of the time, regarded themselves

as their brother-citizens' keepers, freedom, which flourishes
in the indifference of privacy, would be abolished, and
representative institutions would be inundated by the swirl
of plebiscitary emotions—by aggressiveness, acclamation and
alarm.

The first principle of individualist democracy is the partial autonomy of individuals and of corporate bodies or institutions. A very far-reaching degree of autonomy, in adaptation to situations, in the choice of paths of external action,
and internal government, and in the responsibility for unsuccessful choices, is constitutive of freedom. Autonomy should,
however, be partial because it must not be so great as
to obstruct the collaboration of individual with individual,
of individual with institution, and of institution with institution.

Autonomy involves the right to make decisions, to promulgate rules of action, to dispose over resources and to
recruit associates in accordance with criteria which the individual or the organization deems appropriate to its tasks.
The principle of partial autonomy assumes that, by and
large, an individual's or a corporate group's life is its own
business, that only marginal circumstances justify intrusion
by others, and that only more exceptional circumstances justify enforced and entire disclosure, to the eyes of the broader
public, of the private affairs of the corporate body or individual.

Without the willingness to disregard much of what our
fellow citizens do—a disregard based on indifference and
principle—there could be no freedom. In freedom the actions
of the individual or group are unbound by external restraint; in privacy the affairs of the individual or group are
immune from the scrutiny or surveillance of outsiders. Privacy is the voluntary withholding of information. The right
to privacy restricts the power of outsiders to uncover or to
force the disclosure of private matters. Privacy is the antith-
esis of publicity, which is the disclosure of information to a
broad public.

Individualistic or liberal democracy as it has developed

in the West has combined privacy in the affairs which are the business of the individual or a corporate body, with publicity in the affairs of government, which are the business of the citizenry as a whole. Where the affairs of the individual or the corporate body shade off into the sphere of the legitimate concern of the public, the right balance of privacy and publicity becomes a difficult practical problem. The proper principles are, however, clear.

There are many reasons, both in principle and in history, why publicity should have been called to preside over the deeds and intentions of governments. The society which modern democracy superseded throughout most of the Western world was ruled by an absolute monarch or by an aristocracy or a combination of both. The pride of the monarch or the aristocrat forbade the sharing of the knowledge of his actions or intentions with any large section of the population. Indeed, part of the very moral ascendancy and self-esteem of the absolute monarch and the aristocracy lay in their consciousness of possessing *arcana imperium* from which all others in the society were excluded.

This private, unshared knowledge of the art and practice of ruling was both symbolically and factually important for the distribution of power and dignity in the *ancien régime* all over Europe. The struggle for constitutional government, for the extension of the franchise, and particularly for the freedom of the press, which was both an instrument and a symbol in the war against government as a private affair of the monarchy and aristocracy, was directed against privacy in government. Almost as much as the extension of the franchise and constitutional restraint on monarchical absolutism, publicity regarding political and administrative affairs was a fundamental aim of the modern liberal democratic movement. The demand for the publicity of governmental affairs was attended by a demand for the protection and reinforcement of privacy in other spheres—a demand which was itself the child of the aspiration for individual liberty.

To a very great extent, the establishment of the publicity of governmental actions was achieved, as was the corre-

sponding right of the individual to the protection of his
privacy from the surveillance and intrusion of public authority. They were, of course, not achieved completely; for one
thing, aristocratic and oligarchic traditions did not evaporate
entirely and governments were thereby helped in retaining
some measure of confidentiality for their actions. At least as
important, however, in the limitation of the total triumph of
the dual pattern of publicity and privacy, was the recognition that the tasks of government and the obligations of
society did not require or allow their complete fulfillment.

Here and there the right of privacy was infringed on in
the execution of policies called for by public spirit. The
right to privacy could not be completely respected when
taxes were imposed in accordance with capacity to pay,
when civil registration of marriages and births was required,
when members of private associations were to be protected from the financial irresponsibility of their officers, or
when business enterprises sought to establish the personal
reliability of persons appointed to fiduciary positions. The
police in their pursuit of criminals and the judicial system in
its search for trustworthy evidence could not always halt
before the boundaries established by the right of privacy.
On the whole, however, the concern for the social order has,
in modern liberal societies, halted before the boundaries of
legitimate privacy.

It could not be expected therefore that the principle of
publicity could be given an entirely free rein. This not only
because the aristocratic tradition of privacy in governmental
matters was repugnant to publicity. The knowledge of certain governmental transactions had to be confined to a
narrow circle if they were to be effective. Budgetary decisions for example were not given complete publicity prior
to their official release. The deliberations of councils, tri-
bunals and juries had to be protected from premature disclosure. The reports on the affairs of business enterprises
collected in the course of census enumeration or the collection of taxes had to be held confidential. The personnel files
of executive departments, containing many personal details,

could not be subjected to the principle of complete publicity for governmental affairs without intruding still further on the principle of privacy regarding matters which are personal in their essence. Some of these restrictions of public disclosure were maintained because they were called for by the right of privacy already partially infringed on by the government's acquisition of the information.

The needs of government—the *raison d'état*—erected an equally strong bulwark against the total triumph of publicity. Exploratory discussions of domestic policy, in which officials had to state their views with a frankness which would be inhibited if they felt subject to popular misunderstanding and criticism, obviously could not be given publicity even where it was recognized as appropriate for the conclusions reached. Neither in the proposals of alternative policies nor in the analysis of the probable consequences of the various policies would the effectiveness of government be aided by publicity. The very need to retain the co-operation of certain sections of the population who might be alienated by knowledge of what is said about them in preliminary discussions is a curb on publicity in domestic politics and administration.

Raison d'état as a barrier to publicity and a generator of secrecy attained its maximum power in the domain of foreign policy and, above all, of military policy. In that sphere, information about military resources, intentions, strategy and even tactics—in brief, all knowledge and plans about situations in which surprise is important in coping with antagonists—were destined for secrecy. Likewise, the acquisition of the secret information of potential enemies and the network for the acquisition and communication of this information have been acknowledged as fit objects of secrecy. In these fields, secrecy has been accepted in the liberal democracies as a necessary evil. Even the most liberal democratic states have tried to keep these types of information out of the public eye, and not just because military men with their bureaucratic and aristocratic traditions have felt an aversion for sharing their knowledge with civilians, with politicians, businessmen, journalists, and the *hoi polloi.* These motives might have been present, but they were less weighty than considerations of relative military strength which counselled that such information, if it fell into the hands of a potential enemy, would materially reduce the national fighting strength. Even in populistic democracies such as the United States, to the extent that it has been feasible, these matters have often been withheld from the prying press and even from the inquiries of legislators. In any case, military and foreign office officials have sought to keep such knowledge out of the stream of publicity.

What they feared even more than the press, which could be trusted sometimes with a secret given under pledge of confidence, was the spy working for the enemy. The chief protection against the penetration of espionage into vital secrecy was counterintelligence, which sought to identify spies, to lure them into situations in which they could be uncovered and their activities followed out. Efforts were made to penetrate the spy network, to gain the confidence of spies and to discover who their confederates were. This sort of activity had to be kept secret too, for perfectly obvious reasons. Again, although there might be additional professional and caste motives for keeping such work secret, the obvious technical necessity for such secondary secrecy was the overriding factor.

The concern for secrecy, military and diplomatic, was extremely narrow and technical and it was confined to a very limited sphere. It was the preoccupation and responsibility of very few persons. It was a professional responsibility, of which the broader public was usually unaware, and which politicians and the press accepted.

The restriction on publicity imposed by secrecy has by its nature an element of coercion in it. Privacy is the voluntary withholding of information reinforced by a willing indifference. Secrecy is the compulsory withholding of knowledge, reinforced by the prospect of sanctions for disclosure. Both are the enemies, in principle, of publicity. The tradition of liberal, individualistic democracy maintained an equilibrium of publicity, privacy and secrecy. The equilibrium was enabled to exist as long as the beneficiaries and protagonists of each sector of this tripartite system of barriers respected the legitimacy of the other two and were confident that they would not use their power and opportunities to disrupt the equilibrium. The principles of privacy, secrecy and publicity are not harmonious among themselves. The existence of each rests on a self-restrictive tendency in each of the others. The balance in which they coexist, although it is elastic, can be severely disrupted; when the pressure for publicity becomes distrustful of privacy, a disequilibrium results. Respect for privacy gives way to an insistence on publicity coupled with secrecy, a fascination which is at once an abhorrence and a dependent clinging.

II. *The Fascination of Secrecy:*
The Conspiratorial Conception of Society

In the condition of disequilibrium in which publicity destroys privacy, the kind of secret which fascinates and which disrupts is not the technical secret demanded by the *raison d'état*. It is something more ominous, more cosmic in its significance. It is a secret with an aura of fatefulness. It is a secret in which the apocalypse dwells.

It was this other type of secret with which some persons were absorbed in practically all European countries, and in the United States as well, before the first World War. There was a troubled anxiety in some circles about revolutionary activities, carried on away from the public eye. The anxiety attached even to moderate socialist groups in Central and Eastern Europe who were forced at various times in the nineteenth century to carry on many of their quite unrevolutionary activities in a clandestine manner. Revolutionary and terroristic bodies who were forced by their own proclivities and police repression to work in secret were, however, the prime objects of the obsession with the dangers lurking in secrecy.

In aristocratic and *grand bourgeois* circles, the powers of the revolutionary movements were greatly exaggerated, and the alleged secret revolutionary aspirations and preparations of quite harmless reformist organizations became the object of anxious speculation. The occasional assassinations by the Narodniks, by Balkan zealots and much less frequently by French terrorists, bred and supported the worrying belief that hidden away in some sink of society, conspirators were plotting to do away with the existing social order. The sympathy with the national aspirations of the Balkan peoples and with the revolutionary movement in Russia which was common in the educated classes in Western Europe gave a resounding echo to every act of terror and provided the more nervous members of the upper classes with something more to worry about.

This nervousness had a long and well-rooted tradition behind it. For almost a century, substantial sections of the ruling classes in the European continent lived in fear of revolutionary conspiracies.

Towards the end of the eighteenth century, a French clergyman, Abbé Barreul, exiled by the Revolution, gave birth to the notion that the French Revolution had been prepared, organized and executed by the Freemasons. He assembled a vast collection of materials on the history of Jacobinism through which he attempted to demonstrate that the great French Revolution of 1789 had been conceived in advance and thoroughly prepared by a small clique of men operating in secret, hiding their activities from the eyes of their fellow citizens.

The general state of disturbance in other parts of Europe, arising from the French Revolution, elicited similar anxieties. In Germany it was believed that a small sect, consisting mainly of scholars and philosophers, the Illuminati, were planning to subvert the social order. In Italy, the fear of the Carbonari was associated with similar phantasies, and in Russia, naturally, obscurantists in church and state imagined that behind the façade of social order, a complicated conspiracy was afoot, involving far more than students and a few officers. The French Revolution of 1830 and the political clubs of the July Monarchy gave a powerful impetus to the fear of conspiracy. The French Revolution of 1848 as much as any event of the nineteenth century precipitated a generalized anxiety about an endless series of revolutions, produced by hidden cells and conventicles of conspirators. The almost continent-wide upsurge of revolutionary agitation and violence in the same year fortified the inheritance of 1789. The book of a French informer, Lucien de la Hodde's *l'Histoire des sociétés secrètes et du parti républicain en France de 1830 à 1848* (Paris, 1850), in which he laid bare a myriad of conspiratorial and subversive activities, documented these fears and became the *vade mecum* of many a political paranoiac.

The Russian Revolution of October, 1917, gave the greatest sustenance to these worrisome beliefs. The Bolshevik Revolution actually was in part the achievement of a small, tightly-knit body of professional revolutionaries whose seizure of power was possible only through secret machinations. Russia, the homeland of terrorism, now gave birth to the most menacing of modern revolutions. It was the greatest success of a conspiratorial revolutionary body and its resonance in the European and to a much smaller extent, the American labor movements, chilled the blood of persons who were already inclined to worry about the security of their property, and especially of those who feared what they could not see.

The fear of secrecy and conspiracy has been by no means confined to the extremists of conservatism. It is found even more elaborately formulated among the extremists of progress. Ever since the middle of the nineteenth century, the phantasies of the anti-revolutionary extremists have been more than matched by the phantasies, and the doctrine built on them, of the revolutionaries. Less clearly developed in the writings of Marx and Engels, it is in the work of Lenin, particularly in *What is to be Done?*, *The State and Revolution*, and *Imperialism*, that the conspiratorial conception of society is given the form which only a powerful intelligence

could confer on it. In the roughest summary, it states that
bourgeois society is run by a small group of capitalists who
give the orders, make the plans, and in general dominate
every aspect of social, economic, political, and cultural life
in modern society. The Leninist proposition that the state
is the "executive committee of the ruling class," that is the
executive committee of the capitalists, and its contemporary
vulgarization in the argument that Wall Street determines
all that happens in America and among its allies, are manifestations of this hallucination. The phantasy of conspiracy
requires the reality of counterconspiracy so that in the end
the world becomes an arena in which two conspiracies operate, the wicked conspiracy of the enemies and the legitimate
and morally necessary conspiracy of Bolshevism.

In a more general form, the conspiratorial conception of
politics and of society has become one of the commonplaces
of modern fanaticism. The growth of literacy and the extension of the franchise with the accompanying politicization
of the populace has deprived the upper classes of their
monopoly of conspiratorial hallucinations. They have in the
twentieth century also come to be the property of the ideologically inclined in the lower-middle and working classes.
The rural population supplies adherents to the conspiratorial
view of politics no less than the city dwellers.

The belief among Anglophobes and radicals of the extreme left and right that the British Foreign Office really
runs the world and that everyone of its numerous and obvious errors is only a deliberate deception intended to mis-
lead its victims into thinking that they can relax their anxieties, is one of the most common of the conspiratorial
ideas, and it is shared by "right" and "left." Extremist Prot-
estants in the United States in the nineteenth century
thought that secret Roman Catholic societies hiding under
the cover of the church were plotting against the safety of
the United States. Such people believed that the basements
of Roman Catholic churches were arms dumps in which
were stored machine guns, ammunition, grenades and all

that was needed for a new St. Bartholomew's Eve. Even now such conspiratorial fears are occasionally still expressed in extremist Protestant circles. The widespread acceptance in certain circles in the United States and Europe, of the belief that the Elders of Zion sit at the controlling pinnacle of a vast international apparatus which rules much of the world and seeks to rule the rest is another of the conspiratorial articles of faith. Operating from an invisible site and by invisible procedures, the Jews control the doings of bankers and other capitalists as well as Communists and through these reach out to apparently more innocent institutions and strata. The conspiracies often interlock—for many years, there flourished in the Middle West of the United States, the belief that the bankers on the Eastern seaboard were in a secret alliance with the City of London and the British Foreign Office. This fear of the conspiracy of bankers against the rest of society is a common feature of the conspiratorial conception when it becomes populistic. It was found in the National Socialist movement in Germany, in British Fascism, in American populism and more broadly in Bolshevist and Fascist movements in all countries.

The exfoliation and intertwinement of the various patterns of belief that the world is dominated by unseen circles of conspirators, operating behind our backs, is one of the characteristic features of modern society. It is radical in its fundamental distrust of the dominant institutions and authorities of modern society. It is radical in its rejection of the ordinary, matter-of-fact, undramatic, unsystematic outlook of day-to-day politics in the state and in private institutions. It is radical in its denial, explicitly and implicitly, of the reality of the boundaries among institutions and the division of labor which helps to guarantee their autonomy on its more positive side. The conspiratorial conception of society would eradicate the pluralism and privacy of institutions on behalf of a more homogeneous society and a more unitary loyalty. It is not always revolutionary in the conventional sense of planning to supplant the system of private property, but even then it almost always expresses a severe criticism of the property system because it is critical of privacy and the autonomy of institutions.

The main feature of this secrecy-fearing radicalism is its hostility to civil society. Civil society is differentiated and pluralistic; it assumes that citizens will have other concerns than that of continuous and exclusive loyalty to the central authority of the society. Civil society has a large place for the person with a variety of interests and spheres of activity, and whose citizenship is intermittent and interstitial. The very structure of civil society, with its many islands of personal and corporate privacy, is in itself repugnant to the person fearfully preoccupied with the secrets of his enemies and with the need to withhold his own secrets from them.

The political paranoiac imagines that the ultimate seat of conspiratorial evil is almost always outside the *national* community. Because it withholds itself from or is indifferent to complete incorporation into the national community, it is foreign to the national community. Its fundamental foreignness is "demonstrated" by the fact that the conspiracies are ultimately in the control of nationally or ethnically alien groups—Englishmen, foreign capitalists, international bankers, Jews, the Papacy, *et al.*

We should not be understood to imply that all and any aversion to any sort of secret, under any conditions, is necessarily identical with the extremist tradition of the conspiratorial conception of society. There are some kinds of secrecy which from the point of view of civil society are harmful. Conspiracies can exist in society. There are secrets which are necessary. The real difference is between a realistic and an unrealistic view of conspiracy and secrecy, between a sober, businesslike alertness to really dangerous conspiracies and a matter-of-fact protection of necessary secrets on the one hand, and an excited, obsessive, worry about conspiracy and secrecy on the other.

It is not surprising therefore that the fear of conspiracy, in which morally and nationally foreign elements were so central, had, for much of the nineteenth century, little to do with the professional work of counterespionage. Perhaps because of the highly secret nature of the latter field of work and perhaps because of the close-mouthed professional ethos of its practitioners it did not fuse with the more diffuse and less matter-of-fact conspiratorial doctrine of society.

Except in wartime, when one state might wish to profit from subversive and revolutionary movements within an enemy state, there was no interest on the part of spies in stirring up subversion nor did they associate themselves with subversive movements. The professionals of espionage and counterespionage did not moreover think that there was any advantage for revolutionaries to spy for foreign powers.

In general, responsible officials, well- or ill-informed, but usually quite sober, thought that any revolutionary would be opposed, not only to his own government, but to all governments, and that it was therefore most unlikely that he would undertake activities of espionage on behalf of a foreign power. (The occasional revolutionary who became a spy in the pay of the police, confined his espionage to his own revolutionary group and did not spy on governmental secrets.)

III. Secrecy and Publicity

In the pre-Bolshevik era, the interest in the detection of espionage and subversive secrets, held apart from public knowledge as they were, was not attended by a great flurry of publicity. They were, in the main, the object of confidential and secret investigation, and neither the journalists of the elite press nor the journalists of the popular press in the latter part of the nineteenth and earlier twentieth century were particularly concerned with producing great newspaper sensations about revolutionary activities or espionage. Nor were they primarily and continuously concerned, since governmental secrecy was so narrow in its scope, with the unveiling of governmental secrets.

Except for the tiny conventicles meeting in grand salons

and in dingy back rooms where the conspiratorial theory of society flourished, secrecy did not become an obsession. Espionage and counterespionage, although they involved many shady characters and adventurers, were firmly in the hands of professionals who looked on their task as an important job and not as a charismatic mission. The protection of governmental secrets and the penetration of the secrets of subversives and spies was not the preoccupation of many persons who had no professional concern with these activities. The victims of conspiratorial hallucinations had no influence in these circles. Despite certain similarities in the objects of their attention, they were separated by fundamental differences in outlook.

The obsessive concern with the inimical secret occurs in conjunction with blindness to the legitimacy of individual and corporate privacy. It appears together with the restless drive to uncover and disclose. The need to uncover the secrets of others and to keep other secrets within one's own community is a product of the need for unchallenged and unchallenging solidarity. The need to dissolve other people's secrets arises from the need to be surrounded by like-mindedness. The latter need emerges from the anterior need to find support for one's own tendencies of thought and action, dangerously challenged from within, by an environment affirmative of these impulses in oneself which one would like to keep uppermost.

The demand for extreme solidarity is the product of fear of betrayal. Complete and continuous solidarity would obliterate those clandestine activities which, carried on behind one's back, arouse uneasiness over nameless and unnameable dangers. Those who are distressed by divisions in society and who would bring all into the order of uniformity are distressed by the idea that there are secrets of which they know nothing and which can do them harm.

The obsessive fear of secrets culminates in the denial of the right of private difference, which is the denial of the right of others to possess a sphere of privacy. The hatred of the private sphere is a hatred not only of the actions carried out and thoughts harbored in that private sphere, but is also a hatred of the very idea of privacy. When such sentiments are aroused, they lead to intrusions into the private spheres of others. A demand for complete and continuous solidarity cannot be satisfied and cannot rest as long as individuals who are thought to be important for the society retain an unpenetrated sphere of privacy. The hatred of privacy is spawned by the obsession with secrecy. The passion for publicity is the passion for a homogeneous society, a passion which emerges from the conception of politics as the relation between friend and foe. The fear of secrecy is the fear of subversion, and the proper response to the danger of subversion is relentless publicity and a degree of secrecy even greater than the subversives themselves would employ.

Thus the obsessive fear of conspiratorial secrecy is connected with secretiveness, a secretiveness which despite allegations of functional efficiency is enjoyed and revelled in for its own sake. The unrealistic obsession with secrecy—and all its atendant passions for publicity and uniformity—receives a powerful stimulant in a situation in which there is a heightened rational necessity for an efficient and functional system of information security. The existence of a legitimate and rational need for secrecy is tremendously attractive to those who find safety in publicity.

The combination of secrecy which protects and publicity which destroys gratifies the ambivalence which at bottom is characteristic of all extremist orientations. Given the hatefulness and fascination of secrets, the mere idea of persons entrusted with vital, crucial secrets on which the life of the supremely valuable community depends, transforms them into objects of a passionate play of excited sentiment. A great aura of phantasy, of destruction and salvation plays about those who have been entrusted with secrets and whose special knowledge puts them in the position where they must be entrusted with secrets. Since secrecy is so damaging to solidarity the mere possession of the secret gives rise to the suspicion of disloyalty. Hence, their privacy must be dissolved and they must be completely and unreservedly absorbed into an undifferentiated ideological community.

TWO PATTERNS OF PUBLICITY, PRIVACY,

AND SECRECY: THE UNITED STATES

AND GREAT BRITAIN

I. Introductory Remarks

THE PAST DECADE has been the decade of the secret. Never
before has the existence of life-controlling secrets been
given so much publicity and never before have such exertions been made for the safeguarding of secrets. Of the three
great powers, the Soviet Union represents the extreme of
secretiveness. There, publicity is governmentally controlled
and, although used far more widely than in any previously
known oligarchy (for the Soviet Union is, after all, a populistic regime despite the impotence of the populace), it is
used only by the government. It is never used against the
government, and the secrets of the government are immune
from publicity as long as the government wishes to keep
them so. Publicity is directed against malefactors in the government on lower levels and against leaders who have failed.
Privacy in the Soviet Union is not a legitimate area; insofar
as it exists, it exists only on sufferance or out of negligence.
The requirements of secrecy predominate.

The equilibrium of privacy, secrecy and publicity which
has been characteristic of the Western liberal democracies
does not exist in the Soviet Union. Except as a feeble aspiration which never came to life, it never existed in Tsarist Russia. There too governmental secrecy predominated, although
in a far more slipshod manner, and publicity was the timorous
hope of the undeveloped liberal professions. Privacy was the

area of life left over by the negligence and incompetence of the government. But, preoccupied with the fear of revolutionary conspiracies, the government infiltrated much of the society and what would otherwise have been the private zone of many of its members. Tsarist Russia was the only great state of the nineteenth and early twentieth centuries in which the ruling groups were perpetually occupied with the danger of conspiracy. The concern with secrets was an obsessive concern. In Great Britain and the United States the traditions of publicity and privacy were sufficiently strong to hold in check the occasionally surging anxiety about conspiracy. In Great Britain the equilibrium has continued largely intact and, despite minor fluctuations in crises and a long-run trend in favor of increased publicity, it does not seem likely to change greatly in the near future. In the United States it has often verged towards disequilibrium. The disequilibrium is threatened by a continually mounting pressure of publicity and a fluctuatingly powerful preoccupation with secrecy, bound together in the peculiar affinity characteristic of populism under strain.

II. The American Pattern: Luxuriating Publicity

The United States has been committed to the principle of publicity since its origin. The atmosphere of distrust of aristocracy and of pretensions to aristocracy in which the American Republic spent its formative years has persisted in many forms. Repugnance for governmental secretiveness was an offspring of the distrust of aristocracy.

In the United States, the political elite could never claim the immunities and privileges of the rulers of an aristocratic society. Moreover, the suspicion of governmental intentions and the low esteem in which politicians and administrators were held after the Jacksonian revolution lowered the barriers to publicity on the governmental side and increased the insistence on publicity from the side of the governed.

All this occurred before the appearance of the press of

the metropolitan masses. The development of sensational popular journalism coincided with the efflorescence of political and intellectual populism and followed on the flowering of governmental corruption in the tremendous economic expansion of the post-Civil War period. The result was the formation of a tradition of muckraking and exposure of the dark deeds of local, state, and federal governments, and of private business corporations. It was then that the ethos of the American journalistic profession was formed. It viewed the world as its oyster which had only to be pried open to be enjoyed. The ideal of the "scoop" meant that the journalist had always to be on the prowl for undisclosed secrets which would be of interest to his audience—and governmental secrets in an anti-governmental society were always so. American governments in that period offered much that was intriguing in this respect. There was always some corruption or shady dealing at one point or other in the vast, shambling structure of American government, and there was enough disgruntlement and talkativeness among those who had shared in it to reward the inquisitiveness of the journalistic investigator.

Government too marched in tune with the times, for politicians also lived in the tradition of publicity. Congressional investigations fitted perfectly into the populistic pattern of saving the people from the schemes of the powerful. It also met the journalists' need to uncover dark secrets and to assure the populace that their interests were being protected from their enemies in high and remote places.

The First World War, indirectly through the impetus it gave to the study of psychology and directly through the promotion of a belief in the efficacy of propaganda, sent America further into the direction of publicity. In the 1920's, mass production, national prosperity and advertising intensified the pressure for publicity. The growth of mass communications, films, radio and later television, only strengthened and gave new opportunities to a powerful impulse already very well developed.

By the end of the first quarter of the present century, the

principle of aggressive publicity which had become deeply
entrenched over the preceding hundred years thus found a
special professional custodian. The supreme value and self-
constituted task of the journalistic, advertising and mass
communication professions, reinforced by tradition, the
Constitution, and their own professional interests and the
pleasures of professional virtuosity, became the maintenance
and furtherance of publicity. No society has ever been so
extensively exposed to public scrutiny as the United States
in the twentieth century.

The widely ranging freedom of the press has been repeatedly reaffirmed in the United States. The freedom to
comment on court proceedings while a trial is still going on
and the freedom of the press to publish anything it can obtain and to protect its sources are only a few among many
instances of the dominance of publicity in American life.
Few institutions refuse to acknowledge that dominance. Organizations which would appear to gain little from publicity
feel the obligation to have a public relations department;
universities, churches, learned societies accept unquestion-
ingly the importance of "public relations."

The government admits without a qualm the rightfulness
of publicity. The President's press conference, the press conferences of Cabinet officers, fireside chats, even television
broadcasts of cabinet meetings attest the thoroughgoing
permeation of the executive branch by the principle of publicity. Cabinet members and undersecretaries send out with
the aid of ghost writers a continuous flow of articles to the
popular periodicals. Generals, active and retired, find it almost impossible to be silent when so many opportunities in
press, radio and television are offered. And the unending
sequence of dinners of political, professional, religious, and
business organizations gives the executive branch ample
opportunity to spread its views, ill- or well-thought-out, before the nation.

The legislative branch too avails itself of the newest fa-
cilities for diffusing its news while the floors of Congress, not
designed for the most modern forms of publicity, sink into

the background. Congressional debate as a means of instruct-
ing the public yields to television, press conferences, and
radio.

Few voices are raised in criticism of this ocean of publicity, and those which are raised are discredited as soon as
they are heard.

The influence of the Genteel Tradition with its aversion
for publicity suffered a gradual decline concurrently with
the growth of the cultural independence of the Middle and
Far West. The rise into the intelligentsia of the offspring
of the ethnic groups which fell outside the sphere of hegemony of culture of the Eastern seaboard bred a generation in
which restraint was not a virtue, in which distance, deference
and reserve were not esteemed. Self-restraint was equated
with snobbery. The desire for privacy was described as
"stand-offishness." Traditional American friendliness, which
had always been critical of "side," moved with the times
and the decline of etiquette. Traditional American talkativeness by its nature has been inherently antipathetic to
privacy. Talk must have an object—either oneself or the other
person. The need to be in contact and in communication
with the other person is itself a breach in the wall of privacy.

No society could ever eliminate privacy completely.
There are too many inhibitions on the one side and too much
lack of curiosity on the other to permit the private zone
around an individual, a friendship, or a corporate body to
be entirely eroded. American society in the last two decades
has, however, gone very far, certainly further than most
great societies living in the western liberal tradition have
gone. This is by no means without its positive aspect. No
other large-scale society possesses the internal self-percep-
tiveness of American society. The various social classes and
groups are more aware of each other, empathize with each
other more readily and respond more readily to each other's
expectations than in any European society. The whole process of the erosion of privacy and formation of a broad public
sensitivity is to be seen in microcosm in the development of

the social sciences, and especially sociology and social psychology, in the United States.

In the second quarter of the present century, the phenomenal growth of the social sciences, first in University studies and then in lay culture, has accustomed the new educated class to penetration into the privacy of others. Psychoanalysis and even more, its popularization, have had a similar effect. The ethos of an educated class more preoccupied with the observation of their own and other's private selves than any since the flowering of European romanticism, has weakened the barriers against the flood of publicity.

American culture has become "wide open," and any efforts to close it are rearguard actions. There were and are occasional acts of censorship, precipitated by fundamentalists in reaction against modern secular culture, or by the extremists of sexual purity or by one of the great urban churches opposed to the temptations which the modern film or literature places before its parishioners. Even the moral rigorists who espouse suppression and try to enforce it are strong proponents of publicity. Picketing of theaters exhibiting "immoral" films, press conferences and congressional investigations, are characteristic of latter-day efforts to restrict the free movement of the organs of publicity. Even suppression is achieved or sought through publicity.

American culture is a populistic culture. As such, it seeks publicity as a good in itself. Extremely suspicious of anything which smacks of "holding back," it appreciates publicity, not merely as a curb on the arrogance of rulers but as a condition in which the members of society are brought into a maximum of contact with each other. Favoring the exposure of practically every aspect of life, it is uneasy in the presence of those who appear to be withholding something. It is not always tolerant, and its occasional intolerance derives in large part from alarm over folds and convolutions in the fabric of society in which might lie hidden unknown dangers, temptations and disruptions.

This intolerance is by no means incompatible with publicity. On the contrary, publicity is one of the instruments by which populistic intolerance operates.

With its devotion to publicity on such a scale, it could scarcely be expected that in its normal state Americans would have much sympathy with secrecy, particularly governmental secrecy. Within the government, secrecy was at a minimum until the Second World War. Even the military, which in liberal societies is the chief locus of secrecy, was not granted many prerogatives in this respect in the United States nor did it aspire to them. When General Groves, who has played a monumental role in bringing secrecy to the forefront of American consciousness, was asked during the hearings on Dr. Oppenheimer whether he had much experience of security during his army career, he said he had never done so until the Manhattan Project. "The Army as a whole didn't deal with matters of security until after the atomic bomb burst on the world because it was the first time that the Army really knew there was such a thing, if you want to be perfectly frank about it!"

The U. S. Army had very little security training. Soldiers who might be captured in battle were cursorily instructed not to give anything away to their interrogators; there was ample classification and overclassification. There was, however, very little security-consciousness in the Army before the Second World War, and even during the war it was lax. A United States general shortly before D-Day disclosed the date of the attack at a cocktail party in London and his irresponsibility, although not matched, was approached in the general belief that security precautions were a bureaucratic ritual. They were a ritual which had to be observed because security officers could make things unpleasant, but there was little cognizance that the precautions were really necessary.

Within the civilian branches of the government, where secrecy had even feebler roots, "security-consciousness" was very faint.

Without seeking to make a brief for either Mr. John Service, who allegedly passed documents to the staff of *Amerasia,* or for any other American official who has turned confidential documents over to his friends of the press, or who has taken them home or shown them to unqualified persons, it must be remembered that security-consciousness is something new in America. How incomplete it is even now is evident from the continuous flow of inside information in the columns of certain journalists and the premature publication of the Yalta documents because they had obviously been, through some official's own unauthorized decision, placed in the hands of the *New York Times*.

In an individualistic society where the sense of institutional identity is often weak and where the principle of publicity is so central to the national culture, the only relationship between publicity and secrecy would, if men were reasonable, be one of conflict.

The situation is not, however, quite so simple. There are points at which publicity, overreaching itself, also doubles back on itself. At the extremes there is an affinity of opposites. Whereas most Americans take publicity in their stride and are affronted by secrecy, there are some, a small but vigorous minority, who are equally and extremely attracted by both.

There are persons for whom publicity is not just part of the accepted rules of the game of American social life, but to whom it is a means to salvation itself. Like secrecy, which might be functional or magical, so publicity can be practiced and accepted as the normal pattern of relationships among individuals and institutions or it can be endowed with sacred properties and surrounded with excited sentiments.

The American love of publicity is of both types. The former predominates, but there is always a tinge of the latter in it, particularly among the professionals of publicity. In a small sector of the population the balance is reversed and the magical protectiveness of publicity has the upper hand. It is in these circles that the preoccupation with secrecy is greatest—secrecy not in any rational sense, but rather secrecy as a source of danger and as a saving refuge. There is an irrational adhesion of the three elements: fear of secrets, dependence on secrets, and dependence on publicity.

This adhesion has, of course, been sharply catalyzed by the crisis attending the atomic bomb, but it was always a tendency of American populist radicalism of "right" and "left." Populist radicalism of the right has sought its salvation in an all-embracing patriotic homogeneity, within which place has been found for the secrecy of protective organs ranging from the Ku Klux Klan to the Federal Bureau of Investigation and the Atomic Energy Commission.

III. *Hyperpatriotism and the Fear of Conspiracy*

The weaker sense of privacy in America makes for a flimsier attachment to corporate bodies and a fainter assimilation of their traditions. During the Second World War Professor Denis Brogan once said that whenever he was asked by a British civil servant going to Washington for the first time what useful counsel he could offer, he replied that the first thing to bear in mind in confronting an American official was that one was dealing not with the representative of an institution but with an individual. There is, of course, an element of hyperbole in this insight, but it is sound. Institutional loyalties are rather weaker in America than in England. The result is twofold: greater individual expressiveness on the one hand and occasionally a greater responsiveness and intensity of attachment to the more remote national or class or ethnic symbols.

In the United States these broader and yet diverse symbols rise frequently and excitingly to men's minds. Less firmly entrenched in private concerns, attention and sentiment shift easily towards distant public objects. Threats to public objects are envisaged with an almost eager rapidity and "crisis," "crossroads," and "last chances" are too often conjured up when the symbols of the nation come to the fore. There is a close affinity between the idea of the nation and the thought of crisis.

Within professions and professional societies, within occupational groups, within business enterprises, within churches and schools and school systems, and universities, all having their own traditions and their own criteria of recruitment and achievement, their own heroes and ideals, the emergence of an alleged national crisis attenuates autonomy and enfeebles the will to autonomy. At institutional ceremonies and in the internal regulation of institutional life in which the traditions of the institution might be celebrated and honored, there is a tendency in America for the symbols of the nation to come forward and for menaces to its safety to be discussed. At numerous ceremonial dinners, in sermons, at commencement addresses and alumni meetings, at meetings of bar and medical associations, at dedications of buildings and the inauguration of officers of associations, the celebration of the traditions and the past achievements of the club or association or sect are passed over in order to speak at length on the menace presented by America's ceaselessly conniving enemies. Like the Pole who, in the well-known anecdote about the competition for the best essay on the elephant, wrote on "The Elephant and the Polish Question," in the United States there is a perhaps too-ready tendency to invoke the national symbols and give them supremacy over the symbols of private bodies and separate institutions when it is really unnecessary for the well-being and military security of the nation.

Attachment to the most public of symbols, extreme "politicization" to the point of ideological possession, the anchoring of one's soul in the sphere of ultimate politics is the product of a state of mind which sees only white and black. Since all that is not white is not obviously black, it must be "really" black in the sense that it hides its blackness under a disguise. The wicked hide their wickedness under the conspirator's mask of innocence.

Worry about conspiracy has been a constant feature of American life for half a century at least. It has fluctuated in its significance, most of the time remaining the obsession of obscure and uninfluential ranters, but at other times, and especially in the past ten years, rising in intensity and extending its range of influence.

Anxiety about conspiracy brings with it a distortion of the conception of individual responsibility. The peculiar idea of moral infection in consequence of association with individuals of indelible wickedness leads to the notion of "guilt by association." Conspiracy is conceived, not necessarily as oriented towards the performance of specific acts, but as the harboring of certain general states of mind in seclusion or secrecy. The tendency to prosecute for conspiracy has been growing in American practice over the past twenty-five years, a period which coincides with an upward swing of populism. Mr. John Lord O'Brian has observed that "Congress for the past twenty-five years has been consistently endeavoring to establish in our jurisprudence the doctrine of guilt by imputation or belief or 'guilt by association.'" (*Harvard Law Review,* Vol. 61, p. 603.)

The pseudo-crises generated by fears of subversion by secretly working forces are the creations of populist demagogy and they in turn stir up the most stormy passions of populistic demagogy. The demand for complete disclosure, for a complete ironing out of the creases and unevennesses in loyalty to the nation, imposes a great strain on the pluralistic institutional system.

Populistic radicalism almost always harbors, alongside of its fear of secrets, a belief in their salvationary character. In the traditional forms of revolutionary and counterrevolutionary radical populism, the need to keep secrets was concentrated on the inner circle of the conspiratorial band. American populism of the 1940's and 1950's has a new type of secret to engage its feverish worriment and love, namely, scientific secrets.

Science, which for so long had lived apart and to itself, has increasingly in the present century shown how much it could contribute to technology, welfare and defense. In the time of war when all autonomous institutions were being pressed to renounce some of their autonomy, the discovery was made that what science produced could make all the difference to national strength. Under pressure to divulge and not to divulge, science and scientists have fallen into a tormenting cross fire. Offering the quintessence of the most salvationary secrets, scientists have, at the same time and for the same reason, been drawn into the arena of publicity. Never has the tension of secrecy and publicity been so great as it has been in the United States in the past decade, and never has privacy been under such bombardment as since 1945. For almost a decade in the United States the equilibrium of privacy, publicity and secrecy was slipping out of order. It reached a maximum of disequilibrium in the winter and spring of 1954.

A society with as strong a tradition of pluralism as the United States does not lose its equilibrium indefinitely. It has great powers of righting itself. The populistic tendencies of American political sentiment have to contend with the resistance of other tendencies which are just as integral to it. The country has repeatedly shown its capacity to put its wildness behind it—as it did after the flurries of the First World War. And since the summer of 1954 it has once more demonstrated its balancing capacity. The technical problems of secrecy still remain and they are not easy to solve even in the calm light of reason. For the time being, however, the mad passions which endow publicity and secrecy with sacred properties have been repressed. They have been forced back into the lairs where they have always found a home in America, and the normal equilibrium of American life with publicity uppermost has been largely re-established.

IV. The British Pattern:
The Bulwark of Privacy

The equilibrium of publicity, privacy, and secrecy in Great Britain is more stable and its deviations from the normal state are smaller than they are in the United States. Like America, Great Britain is a modern, large-scale society with a politicized population, a tradition of institutional pluralism, a system of representative institutions and great freedom of enquiry, discussion and reporting. Like America, it also has a sensational popular press which goes to the limits in the infringement of privacy—limits which are narrower in Great Britain than in the United States. It also produces demagogues of great oratorical gifts, capable of arousing political passions and, as in the United States, they seldom attain the highest positions of authority. Yet this tells us very little about Great Britain because the differences are considerable. Despite occasional outbursts of acrimony and gross abuse, British political life is strikingly quiet and confined. Modern publicity is hemmed about by a generally well-respected privacy. Secrecy is acknowledged and kept in its place.

Although democratic and pluralistic, British society is not populist. Great Britain is a hierarchical country. Even when it is distrusted, the Government, instead of being looked down upon, as it often is in the United States, is, as such, the object of deference because the Government is still suffused with the symbolism of a monarchical and aristocratic society. The British Government, of course, is no longer aristocratic. Only the House of Lords remains, although in a greatly diminished form, as an instrument and symbol of aristocratic prerogative. The members of the Government come from all classes, primarily from the middle and upper-middle classes, but they participate in a set of institutions which has about it the aura of aristocracy and it enjoys therefore the deference which was given to that aristocracy. It enjoys the deference which is aroused in the breast of Englishmen by the symbols of hierarchy which find their highest expression in the Monarchy. Although the British Government is as democratic as any in the world, the institutions through which the Government operates still enjoy the respect which their aristocratic incumbents once aroused and which connection with the Crown still confers.

British participation in political life is somewhat greater than participation in the United States, but it does not express populist sentiments. The mass of the politically interested citizenry does not regard itself as better than its rulers. In contrast with the United States, the mandatory conception of the legislator does not find much support in Britain outside a small and radical section of the Labour Party. The ordinary citizen does not regard his own judgment as better than, or even as good as, his leaders'.

Walter Bagehot said many years ago that the English Constitution worked because the English were a deferential people. England has undergone many changes since Bagehot wrote; the peerage has been brought down, the Court is no longer so prominent and the great London houses have descended from their glory. The distribution of opportunity is far more equalitarian now than it was in 1867, and organizations supported by the working classes share in the power to an extent which seemed impossible at that time. But in the distribution of deference, Britain remains a hierarchical society.

The acceptance of hierarchy in British society permits the Government to retain its secrets, with little challenge or resentment. The citizenry and all but the most aggressively alienated members of the elite do not regard it as within their prerogative to unmask the secrets of the Government, except under very stringent and urgent conditions. For the same reason, the populace is ordinarily confident that their rulers can be counted upon to keep secret that which has to be kept secret.

The deferential attitude of the working and middle classes is matched by the uncommunicativeness of the upper-middle classes and of those who govern. The secrets of the governing classes of Britain are kept within the class and even within more restricted circles. The British ruling class is unequalled in secretiveness and taciturnity. Perhaps no ruling class in the Western world, certainly no ruling class in any democratic society, is as close-mouthed as the British ruling class. No ruling class discloses as little of its confidential proceedings as does the British. The televising of a cabinet meeting, such as happened recently in the United States, was profoundly shocking to British political circles.[1]

---

1. The dominance of public events in British political life by television engineers and camera men as has happened on various occasions in the United States, is quite inconceivable.

The broadcast of the proceedings of a Parliamentary Committee or a Royal Commission would not be tolerated in Great Britain. Even the wireless discussion of issues about to come before Parliament is regarded as an intrusion into the autonomous sphere of the House of Commons. Even the most central public bodies are regarded as having an appropriate privacy which must be respected.

In contrast with the United States, where government documents are made available to historians without long delay, in Britain governmental papers which are not published at the time as part of government policy, are opened to scholarly inspection only after a very long lapse of time and even then with restrictions. Government officials, Cabinet ministers and their biographers always tread with discretion in personal and political matters. Again the contrast with America is very great. The memoirs of American political figures, although not always entirely written by themselves, disclose far more of the inner workings of party, government, and department than is the case in Britain. Only on very rare occasions does a British public figure, in his autobiography, make personal remarks disclosing his opinion of his fellow politicians or officials. There is practically no book in the modern literature of British political autobiography comparable to the late Harold Ickes' recent autobiographical works in which rivals are excoriated and enemies denounced in a language of extraordinary harshness. It is not that British politicians do not have animosities and mean thoughts of their colleagues and opponents. They have them in ample measure, but the rules of privacy forbid their public expression, beyond a narrow circle of equals.

What is spoken in privacy is expected to be retained in privacy and to be withheld from the populace.[2] When journalists are confided in, it is with the expectation that the confidence will be respected. "Government by leaks" in Great

---

2. The journalist who discloses what is said behind the wall of privacy breaks the rules. He arouses the resentment of those on the "inside" and the curiosity of those on the "outside," but in both circles he is known to be doing the unusual thing.

Britain is extremely infrequent. It is not a technique of warfare of one department against another or of one official against another.

The traditional sense of the privacy of executive deliberations characteristic of the ruling classes of Great Britain has imposed itself on the rest of the society and has established a barrier beyond which publicity may not justifiably penetrate. Nowhere is this more evident than in the conduct of the British press, through which the impulse towards publicity is expressed.

The press in Great Britain, with all its vulgarity and all its curiosity about the great, keeps its place. For all the criticism of the Government of the day, the press maintains its distance and seldom pries into the affairs of the bureaucracy. Certainly it never comes anywhere near the practice of the American press in such matters. Sensational though much of the press is, it seeks sensations of unveiled privacy in the main elsewhere than in the disclosure of the vices of government. Muckraking in the American style is not one of the features of the British press, even the most sensational type. The exposures of governmental misdeeds featured in the British press are largely those uncovered by the Opposition or by some meticulously conscientious member of the Government. It is only then that political scandal-mongering is rendered legitimate.

The awe of the press before the majesty of Government is expressed also in the silence of the press about cases under trial in the courts. Whereas in the United States, the newspaper treatment of trials may involve editorial comments on the issues and parties, interviews with some of the principals and even analysis of the jurors and their deliberations, in Great Britain the newspapers must acquiesce in the exclusion of these areas from the scope of their professional virtuosity.

The British journalist, in his dealings with the government, handles himself as if he were an inferior of the person clothed with the majesty of office. His esteem for his own profession does not permit him to look on judges, members of Parliament and civil servants as if they were dependent upon him for publicity which he had in his power to give or withhold. Politicians in Great Britain like publicity, but their conception of what is possible and permissible usually falls within fairly narrow limits. The press conference plays a far smaller part in Whitehall and Westminster than it does in Washington. The balance of power between Government and the press favors the Government in Great Britain and the press in the United States.

In this manner, publicity in Great Britain is held in check. The Governments of Great Britain are not secretive in the way of an absolutist regime. Parliamentary debates are more fully reported than are Congressional debates in the United States and they are more widely discussed. A continuous flow of White Papers, Royal Commission Reports, Select Committee Reports, etc., throw light on the action and intentions of the Government. In the main, journalists are content to leave it at that. The secrets of the Government are not only protected by an Official Secrets Act and the strong silencing sense of corporate obligation on the part of ministers and civil servants; they are sustained too by the journalists' restraint in the presence of Governmental secrecy.

The professionals of publicity, political and journalistic, not being quite so fascinated by the secrets of the Government, do not feel their integrity and status dependent on the unravelling of secrets. Accordingly, they do not, like some American populist publicists and politicians, act as if salvation depended on secrecy as well as publicity. Very few strong complaints were made in Britain in 1948 that the Government's newly stated policy for keeping "security risks" out of sensitive positions was not sufficiently stringent. The defection of Maclean and Burgess, scarcely more than the misdeeds of Fuchs, Nunn May and Pontecorvo did not rouse a great outcry in Britain for far more stringent restraints on those entrusted with secrets.[3] There was practi-

---

3. It is possible that the slackness of British security which allowed Burgess and Maclean to escape notice so long arose from the mutual confidence of the different sectors of the ruling classes.

cally no demand for stricter measures against civil servants; the recent decision of the Government to increase the number of sensitive positions from which Communists would be excluded was not the product of popular pressure, in the House of Commons or in the press or in any organizations. Miss Rebecca West's suggestion that scientists have a special disposition towards treason found a louder echo in the United States than in Great Britain.

Secrecy is less fascinating in Great Britain because privacy is better maintained and publicity less rampant. The balance produced by the moderation of the demand for publicity, respect for the integrity of secrets and insensitivity to the magic of secrecy rests then on hierarchy, deference and self-containment. Self-containment is a part of the pluralism of British society.

By pluralism we mean the firm attachment and simultaneous and intermittent loyalty to a plurality of corporate and primordial bodies; to family, profession, professional association, regiment, church, chapel, club, and football team, political party, friends, and nation. Pluralism entails the more or less simultaneous exercise of attachments to these diverse objects and the maintenance of a balance among them so that none is continuously predominant. It is not rootlessness. On the contrary, it depends on solid bonds, on the enjoyment of traditions and the belief in the supra-individual character of the institution and of the members' obligations to them. But it does not permit such a degree of absorption into any one of the groups that members would be blind to the claims and values of the others.

It is the reverse of specialization of interest and concentration of loyalty. In Great Britain, politics, ideally and in practice, is not permitted to claim all of an individual's attention. Naturally, the politician will usually prize political activity above most others, but he will feel compelled to show an interest in other fields of activity as well and to show himself to be a well-rounded human being. The scientist is expected not to allow science to rule out every other interest or concern. The situation is the same in other professions. The multiplicity of interest which this standard maintains in each individual means that passions are less frequently absorbed by single objects. In consequence, fanaticism appears less frequently in British ruling circles in the twentieth century than it does in many other modern countries. The reality of the propertied and leisured classes, devoting themselves in an amateur way to politics, sports and philanthropy, scarcely exists any longer in Great Britain, but the tradition which it set going, however, is still a force among men whose condition in life is very different.

The tradition of the amateur, with its aversion to specialization, is a major constituent in the internal solidarity of the British ruling classes, regardless of their class of origin. It promotes amicable relations within the elite and amicable dispositions and a ready empathy with one another. Mutual trust reduces the fear of secretiveness and the need for publicity. In such a situation there is less fear on the part of sensitive persons that secrets are being kept from them. The feeling of affinity which members of the elite in Great Britain have towards one another, the feeling of proximity and of understanding which they have for one another despite all disagreements and antagonisms, restrains the tendency to fear hidden secrets. It increases the acceptability of secrecy within the elite since it symbolizes an acknowledgment of equality. By increasing the solidarity of the elite it increases the capacity to keep secrets within the group and reduces the disposition to "leak" secrets in order to show "outsiders" that one is "on the inside." The internal solidarity and mutual confidence of the elite is accompanied by a greater insensitivity to the sentiments of those outside.

The respect for one's "betters" and the mutual trust within the ruling classes are infused with a general disposition towards a lack of interest in the private affairs of the next man. In all classes of the population in England, men can live close to one another, work with one another and even be friends for a long time while remaining quite ignorant of each other's affairs and past. This ignorance is partly a function of indifference, partly of tact and the belief that the other's affairs are his own business.

There is less active curiosity in England on the part of one individual about another. There is less probing, there is less quick empathy, and less readiness to imagine oneself into the state of mind of another person. The general lack of social understanding, the ignorance of the social structure of Great Britain which one finds in so many sections of the British population—the blindness about British society which one finds in the educated classes—means that alongside of the broad sense of unity, which reduces anxiety, there is also a lower level of mutual, imaginative penetration and less of an impulse to penetrate into the interior life of other persons.

This does not mean that there is not gossip, often of a very malicious sort, or that there is not pathological curiosity, a considerable market for literature about the private life of the royal family, or a considerable audience for scandal from the divorce courts. England has all of these. But they all exist within the matrix of a quite striking acceptance of the legitimacy of the privacy of one's fellow man. The person who keeps to himself in Britain will be less criticized than he would be in America. This difference in the sense of privacy contributes to the maintenance of the equilibrium by offering resistance to pressures for publicity and for the search for salvation in the opposite of publicity, namely, the concentration of secrecy.

Through the spirit of privacy, the deferential attitude towards government is reinforced. If anybody in Britain would have grounds to feel that the ruling group was secretive, it would be the lower and middle classes who are so excluded from "inside" knowledge. Much more is withheld in Britain than in America from the scrutiny of the public. Yet the ruling classes in Great Britain are respected, and they are entitled, in the eyes of the mass of the population (lower-middle class and working class, rural and urban) to possess their secrets as long as they are not obviously harming anyone. Thus the circle is turned, and an equilibrium of secrecy, privacy, and publicity kept stable.

Although the British and the official spokesmen of their corporate institutions are much afflicted with national conceit, on the whole they are less preoccupied with the symbols of nation and of national unity than some of the more vociferous Americans. Those who are so preoccupied get less of a hearing and are less influential. On ceremonial occasions, the national symbols are less frequently invoked and less intensely invoked in Great Britain than in America. In the United States a trade or professional association, being addressed at a conference, is more likely to learn about the threat of Communism and the needs of national defense. In Great Britain this is less likely to be so. The fact of nationality lies less continuously and less restlessly on the minds of the British upper and upper-middle classes. It is not that there are not in all political positions in Great Britain, hyperpatriots who refer everything they discuss to a British standard and find it wanting. There are many Englishmen, especially since the war, who have Britain on their minds over all else. But they do not, on the surface at least, seem to be defending themselves from external attack. British jingoism does not seem to be in such need of the internal homogeneity of society as its American counterpart. American hyperpatriotism seems always to call for loyalty, maximal loyalty, while British national conceit is capable of being unworried by the internal heterogeneity of British society. The British phenomenon is directed towards foreigners; the American towards other Americans as well as foreigners.

Feeling less exposed to attack from hidden enemies allied to external enemies, there is less need for publicity to root them out and to uncover their secrets. Less preoccupied with secrets and indeed accepting a mild type of secrecy as a normal mode of life, there is more confidence that such secrets as are deemed necessary will not be stolen or disclosed with harmful intentions. Just as the British are less perceptive of crises than the Americans and more apt to deny their existence, while the Americans tend to overemphasize them, so British security measures tend towards an overconfident and gentlemanly laxity and inefficiency, while

American security measures tend towards excessive and unnecessary rigidity and comprehensiveness.

The two patterns which we have just described have
much in common. It would be impossible for two large-scale,
highly industrialized, highly democratic liberal countries to
exist at opposite poles. In each of the countries there is
normally an equilibrium of publicity, privacy, and secrecy.
Each of the countries has, however, a somewhat different
weighting of the elements. In America it is publicity, in
Britain privacy, and even a matter-of-fact, unemotional, un-
magical secrecy which weigh a lot more heavily than the
other elements in the culture. In America, for the balance to
be maintained, there must be a perpetual struggle to keep
publicity and a nervous worry about secrets, good and bad,
from inundating individual and corporate privacy. In Britain the equilibrium requires a constant alertness lest the
privacy of the upper stratum in government and culture
proves too great a bulwark against publicity.

The specifically British disequilibrium, which is restricted
in range, is the preponderance of privacy and traditional
governmental secretiveness over publicity. The specifically
American disequilibrium is the preponderance of publicity
and its attendant stress on salvationary secrecy over privacy.

PART II

The Background
of Excess

CHAPTER 3

THE CHANGING WORLD

I. Introductory Remarks

THE COMMUNIST PARTY of the United States is and has been malevolent in intent. Its impotence as an effective conspiratorial revolutionary body does not mean that it is entirely harmless. Given the interest of the Soviet Union in penetrating such information on American resources and intentions as are kept secret, and given the subservience of the Communist Party to the Soviet Union, there have been ample grounds for care in dealing with Communists or persons under their influence. The maintenance of a reasonable degree of secrecy in military technology and in the formation of our foreign and military policy is necessary. As long as the present system of international relations continues, the reality of the threat of espionage is great enough to merit responsible thought and action.

The furor in the United States about secrecy and conspiracy has, however, gone beyond the point requisite for a reliable system of security.

Why has a legitimate concern with security become so distorted and inflated? Why has it pursued so many false pathways? Why is there so much activity which alleges to add to the security of our secrets but which adds so little? Why has such a considerable fraction of our federal Congress, over so long a period, and so many of our state legislatures, given so much of their attention to security problems which are in fact only indirectly related to the real and legitimate task of security? Why have so many of our citizens been so preoccupied with thoughts of subversion, spying and secrecy? Why, for so long, did so many of our journalists in print, radio, and television, devote so much time to the problems of Communist conspiracy and infiltration and the battle against them? Why have so many of our school boards, our clergy and the legal profession and so many leaders of so many of our professional and civic bodies worried so much about the dangers of Communism in America?

The sources of this cancerous deformation of a just concern lie in the world and in ourselves. The situation in world politics—the changes in the distribution of power in the world, in our position in that distribution, and in the burdens imposed on us by the position we have partly aspired to and partly have had thrust upon us—have contributed greatly. There are not less significant factors within ourselves—in our own society and in our traditions, in our long-persisting attitudes towards government, learning and the great world— which have brought us into a disgraceful morass of inefficiency, irrationality and self-deception in our security policy.

It is common to point out that the American people have quickly adjusted themselves to the responsibilities of power. This is true, but it fails to state that the adjustment has been accompanied by much friction. The preoccupation with secrecy and conspiracy is one of these frictions—although it is, paradoxically, also one of the additional stimulants to the effort which has gone into the adjustment.

The ready acceptance of the tasks of international collaboration and opposition—the traditional tasks of all foreign policy—by one large section of our population has aroused in those who do not quite accept the tasks, a sequence of energetic reactions. These reactions draw their direction and strength from many older American attitudes. The energy of the reaction flows through many devious channels, and strange and indirect confluences emerge.

II. Insolubility

The problems created for America by the movement of world politics towards bipolarity have been fiercely troublesome because they have provided no prospect of an ultimate

and reasonable solution. The Soviet Union has not been conciliatory, and such is its reputation that when it appears to
be conciliatory it is even more suspect. The Soviet Union
has expanded in territory and influence, first in Europe and
then in Asia in a manner which has offered no prospect of
cessation. Except for Britain, our allies are weak or half-
hearted, and India's neutrality has been disquieting and
exasperating. The aggressiveness of the Soviet Union is aggravated by the existence of parties in nearly all non-Soviet
countries of Europe and Asia which press the Soviet line,
agitate for it, spy for it, sabotage for it, and who, in brief,
are organized agents of Soviet foreign policy—and who in
one way or another are tolerated and even applauded in
countries which purport to be our allies.

Such a situation would have been troubling enough before the atomic bomb. The crisis in Europe occasioned by
the rise of Nazism precipitated a great conflict in the United
States between "internationalists" and "isolationists" and
brought with it many elements of the present preoccupation
with secrecy and subversion.

Before the war the Soviet Union was not our enemy and
it was much weaker. There was no atomic bomb. The same
sentiments were there, however, less intense and less clamorous.

Now there are uncontrolled nuclear weapons on both
sides. There is no certain safety from Soviet espionage. The
Soviet Union is here to stay, and so is Soviet China, and they
are not to be wished or propagandized out of existence. This
is unpleasantly present in the minds of many of those who
hate these regimes most.

The menace of destruction, more imminent than ever, can
be guarded against, but without any assurance of success.
The tremendous armament burden has given no prospect of
diminution. The United Nations has brought no easement.
The arena of international politics into which Americans
have entered by virtue of the accidents of history and geog-
raphy, by no means entirely by their own will, and from

which they cannot withdraw as long as they prize the honor and power of their country, has allowed no definitive solutions. It has allowed only an endless, incessant struggle to keep ahead of every potential enemy or coalition of enemies. It has meant accumulating weapons and the knowledge which can help to make weapons. Those who are sensitive, rationally or irrationally, to the facts of international politics, know that the Soviet Union is skillful in science and technology. The fact that a few of the irrationally hypersensitive think that Soviet weapons were stolen from the United States with the collusion of Americans, although not a widespread belief in its most extreme form, has added to the stress. This mad belief coalesced with the irrational fear that, even if it has not yet happened, it might happen at any time.

This dim, prospectless outlook has been hard to take for people to whom most problems of human organization, technique and social relations had hitherto seemed soluble.

It is not just the fact that the American people and their leaders are new to the world of realistic international politics. They are relatively new, it is true, but it is no less true that a large part of the strain comes from the unprecedented difficulties of bipolarity and the extraordinary destructiveness of modern weapons. The dangers of a lost war are not merely humiliation and impoverishment; they are sheer destruction of much of the urban population and the utter destruction of the physical assets of the country as well as its disintegration as a state and as a society. The existence of such weapons in the hands of a relentless enemy, with its secret allies in our midst, would necessarily be very disquieting, even to calm minds used to accepting the existence of a crisis only gradually and skeptically. America is not traditionally a country which underestimates crises—and the present situation is certainly not one which even the most serene minds can view with equanimity. It is strenuous to be endangered and incapable of ending the crisis; it is infuriating to feel that what one holds sacred is rendered insecure by hidden enemies who through indifference or design would give away the secrets on which survival rests. This emotional state could scarcely do other than make for receptiveness to agitation about secrets and about the Communists and their witless pawns who would steal them.

III. Dreams of Peace and Harmony:
Disillusionment

Ten years ago, as the war was coming to an end, the United States was in a quite different state of mind. The triumphant outcome of the war was certain, but the aftermath was still very unclear. The anxiety of personal separation and personal danger was supplanted by anxious hopes and fears for the future of the world.

With a rush, American idealism reached out towards the world as an object to be embraced and led. The idea of a world in which America accepted the responsibilities of its power was taking form. It was the image of a world united in the United Nations, with dependent and subject peoples liberated, with America taking the lead as a benevolent, generous, and monitory guide to the rest of the world, which would give up its wicked ways. Many, and not just fellow travellers or Communists, hoped and therefore thought that the Soviet Union could be brought to give up its surly diplomacy and its revolutionary incendiarism and allow the virtues, in which many wished to believe, to come to the fore.

This conciliatory attitude towards the Soviet Union was not universally or unambivalently shared in the United States. There were those who did not feel such an effort should be made because they hated the Soviet Union and were convinced that no good could come of treating with it.

Those who disapproved of the outstretched hand were the prewar isolationists, reinforced now by the Polish-Americans, the Hungarian-Americans, the Irish-Americans, and in general those related to the nations and the church which had been despoiled by the Soviet Union in its expansion into central and eastern Europe. Except for the Communists and their friends, most of the others who wished to extend a conciliatory hand towards the Soviet Union did so with misgivings. They did not feel confident, but they thought that the effort should be made.

Nonetheless, despite misgivings and hesitation there can be no doubt that there were features of Russian life which many apolitical and political Americans liked and thought were virtues. The freedom from formality and the spontaneous warm-heartedness of the Russians met during the war entered into the American conception of Russia. It found its counterpart in the American dislike of ceremonial and hierarchy. Informality, cheerfulness, vigorous drinking and emotional outgoingness often appears to Americans to be democratic, in part, perhaps, because it diverges so widely from what "grass-roots" Americans regard as aristocratic, snobbish and British.

At the end of the war, even internationalist Americans—except for those who were hard-headed enough to foresee the necessity of the Anglo-American alliance and those who were simple Anglophiles—were not very happy about Great Britain. The Prime Minister had asserted that he did not intend to preside over the dissolution of the Empire. The British were aiding the Dutch in Indonesia and even worse, they were aiding the Greek Government against the Communist section of the resistance movement. The populistic anti-imperialism which is characteristic of both the internationalist and isolationist strands of American political sentiment was galvanized against the British for their intervention in the Greek disorder, and Soviet propaganda and its Communist echo in the United States were exploiting it to try to break the intimate connection between the United States and Great Britain.

In contrast with Britain, the Soviet Union added to the virtue credited to it by its courageous war against the Germans, by passing as an anti-imperialist power. It had no obviously ill-gained territorial acquisitions to yield in the general liberation of the peoples for which internationalists hoped and isolationists insisted.[1] An American prejudice that imperial aggrandizement at the cost of adjacent, formerly independent areas, once accomplished, is legitimate or may at least be forgotten while expansion into distant areas is illegitimate, coincided with the parallel Marxist prejudice. This coincidence, which is only one of the many shared by Marxism and American populism, made the Soviet Union appear, in contrast with Britain, to be utterly unimperialistic, and thus very much like the United States.

The difference in governmental systems and in the underlying ethos of the two systems did not trouble most Americans at this time. Mr. Henry Wallace's report on his journey to the Soviet Union expressed sentiments which were not alien to the American state of mind at that time.[2] The reasons for the affinity of Mr. Wallace's views of the Soviet Union and popular sentiment persist, although Mr. Wallace and his appreciation of the Soviet Union have long since been rejected, because both expressed the utopian, equalitarian populism, which in its anti-Communist manifestation underlies much of our present preoccupation with secrecy and conspiracy.

IV. *The Atomic Bomb and the Secret*

Every strain of the postwar world has been accentuated by the atomic bomb. What would have been a very difficult situation has been made far more difficult. It created a situation to which the best diplomacy might never have been equal, and to which Soviet obstinacy and distrust and American uncertainty—both deformed by the temptations of publicity—were certainly unequal. The uncontrolled atomic bomb and its latter-day fellow, the hydrogen bomb, have

---

1. For obvious reasons of language and politics, the Ukrainians had never been able to win the sympathy of the American people for the struggle for Ukrainian national autonomy in the way the Irish and the Indians had.

2. Mr. Wallace's obduracy and persistence in that point of view long after he had fallen out of line with the prevailing trend of American opinion finally completed his political ruin.

accentuated beyond measure the difficulties of stabilizing the world order and of maintaining internal serenity in the United States.

The atomic bombs which fell on Hiroshima and Nagasaki were hailed with happy bewilderment by the American people, for they ended the war and gave evidence of American greatness in a sphere most valued in America — in the application of scientific knowledge. For most people in 1945 the chief significance of the bomb consisted in having brought the end of the war and with it the return to private life and civilian interests in a society which had unwillingly been forced to live too much in the presence of great events. They embraced the bomb and peace together.

But the bomb left in its wake grave apprehensions which soon became substantial. The faint trace of guilt which was tinting the outlook of some Americans has never really died away, but it has been greatly overshadowed by a far more widespread horror over any future use of the bomb. Throughout those parts of the population which can bring themselves to think a little about the atomic and thermonuclear bombs there is a deep feeling of abhorrence, coupled usually with an acceptance of their necessity in the present situation.

After the first excitement, attention was dispersed to return at especially worrying moments, and those sections of the population which were more sensitive to the events of the larger world—the professional politicians, the ideological extremists, the morally hypersensitive and the scientists—were left in charge of America's conscious thought and sentiment about the atomic bomb. It was inherent in the situation that "the secret" soon became the central issue.

The scientists, who had worked on the bomb and knew its monstrous powers, felt perhaps more than a little guilty over their role in having produced this necessary tool of destruction and they also knew enough about the inner nature of science and scientists to foresee that the American monopoly of the scientific and technological knowledge which went into the making of the bomb could not be indefinitely maintained. The years in which the monopoly could last, they insisted, were few, and even the military men who worked with the scientists acknowledged this, with some reluctance. For this reason many of the scientists, with a hopeful pessimism, supported the establishment of a system of international control which would both protect America and keep atomic bombs from being used.

The Administration which shared the scientists' views proposed, in the Acheson-Lilienthal Report and in the Baruch Plan, a method of control which would both maintain American security for a fairly long period and which also acknowledged the inevitable loss of the American monopoly in scientific knowledge and technology. The project envisaged the gradual dissolution of the secret. The supporters of international control were attacked on the one side by the Communists and their accomplices, who wished the United States to destroy its stockpile of atomic bombs at once, and a small non-Communist group which demanded an immediate end to secrecy. From another side the Administration and its scientific and political advisors were subjected to harsh attacks for their readiness to renounce the vital secret on which America's future depended. The scientists' conviction that even perfect secrecy would not guarantee the monopoly indefinitely was transformed, by those to whom secrecy had the titillating effect of catnip on a kitten, into the statement that any secrecy was pernicious and should be forthwith removed.

The debate about salvation through secrecy or its renunciation had scarcely begun in the United States when the British Government, on March 4, 1946, announced the arrest of Alan Nunn May and then proceeded, on May 1, 1946, to convict him for the transmission of information about the atomic bomb to the Soviet Union. The Canadian Government announced on February 15, 1946, the arrest of twenty-two persons for the transmission of secret information to a foreign power. Through the rest of the year the Canadian government was trying and convicting many of these persons. The Canadian spy ring and its use as a base for obtaining American and Canadian atomic energy secrets continued to be featured in the press for many months. In 1946 Carlo Marzani, a minor State Department employee, was indicted and sentenced for perjury in denying that he had been a member of the Communist Party. In 1948 the heavy artillery went into operation. Miss Elizabeth Bentley and Mr. Whitaker Chambers began their series of public revelations about Communist espionage in the United States Government. At the end of 1948, after much publicity, Alger Hiss was indicted for perjury. It was not his perjury, but rather his espionage, that interested the politicians and the political public—espionage on behalf of the Soviet Union at a time when Soviet atomic energy espionage was on people's minds.

At the same time it had become perfectly clear in the United Nations Atomic Energy Commission that the Soviet Union would not participate in a feasible and effective system of the international control of atomic energy. The American visage began to cloud over. Secrets were to become our chief reliance just when it was becoming more and more evident that the Soviet Union had long maintained an active apparatus for espionage in the United States. For a country which had never previously thought of itself as an object of systematic espionage by foreign powers, it was unsettling.

The world was not working as it had been hoped. The Soviet Union was obviously not allowing itself to be moved by dreams of a world of peace and mutual aid. The Soviet vetoes began to pile up in the Security Council of the United Nations. The country was forced to make more and more explicit its alliance with Great Britain, and this did not please those who, while hating the Soviet Union, also hated Great Britain as well. When Mr. Churchill came to Fulton in 1946 and delivered his great address on the need for an Anglo-American alliance, it appeared to be another of the serpentine British Foreign Office's efforts to engage America once more in Europe's ancient and unending quarrels.

Neither isolationists nor internationalists liked the prospect offered by Mr. Churchill.

In this crisis, the possession of a vital secret became the straw of the drowning man. The retention of the vital secret became the focus of the phantasies of apocalypse and destruction, of the battle between the children of light and the children of darkness, which Western Christian society has inherited from ancient and medieval dualistic heresies. These ideas re-emerge, in secular and religious forms, in periods of distress and they offer salvation, which may be achieved either through revolution or through return to the "good old days."

In America, dualistic extremism was part of the Puritan heritage, and it later found a home in the Middle West where fundamentalism and populism were to be counted among its offspring.

The atomic bomb was a bridge over which the phantasies ordinarily confined to restricted sections of the population, —hole-and-corner nativist radicalism, religious fundamentalism and revolutionary populism—entered the larger society which was facing an unprecedented threat to its continuance. The phantasies of apocalyptic visionaries now claimed the respectability of being a reasonable interpretation of the real situation.

V. The Danger of Subversion by Infiltration: Czechoslovakia and Miss Bentley

1948 was an important point in the development of the postwar preoccupation with subversion and secrecy. An earlier notice had been given by the Soviet Union in its treatment of Poland and Hungary, actions which had both hurt the American conscience and stimulated strongly anti-Communist sentiment among Americans of Polish and Hungarian extraction. Towards the end of the winter of 1948, the Communist Party in Czechoslovakia seized power through a *coup d'état*. By the threat of violence and its domination of police and army, achieved through control of the Ministries of Defense and Interior, and through its occupation of the key positions in trade unions, the Czechoslovak Communist Party was able to force the President to create a Communist cabinet and to forestall the coming elections.

The Czechoslovak Republic was a favorite of the United States. It had been created under American blessing. Its first two Presidents had lived in the United States, preparing themselves for their return, during the two World Wars. It had been the victim of what most Americans abominated: it had been immorally sacrificed by the laborers in the vineyard of Munich and then when rendered powerless it had been seized by the Nazis. It was, moreover, supported by a powerful Czech community in the United States, almost entirely anti-Communist.

Just as the Moscow trials of the 1930's and the Soviet-Nazi Pact of 1939 had settled the minds of some wavering Communist Party members and fellow-travellers against the Soviet Union, so the Communist *coup d'état* in Czechoslovakia settled the minds of many postwar Soviet sympathizers in the United States after the war. It was a definitive notification that the Soviet Union did not mean even to give the pretense of being amiable.

On April 1st of the same year, further notification was delivered with the blockade of Berlin, but of the two foreign events of 1948 the Czech coup was more drastic in its impact on American opinion. For one thing, in the Berlin blockade we could fight back, and we finally broke the blockade in a completely unambiguous manner. The success was a characteristically American success of skill in organization and personal daring. In the Czech coup we could not fight back against the aggressors—there were no aggressors to fight against. Soviet troops had not played any tangible part in the Communist seizure of power. It was ostensibly an entirely internal matter. There had not even been any violence. Through their control of the trade unions and the Ministries of Defense and Interior, into which they had judiciously installed themselves at the end of the war, and through a characteristic Socialist fear of offending the Communists, the Communists were able to impose themselves on President Benes and the Czech people in a pseudo-constitutional manner. It was a triumph of the tactics of the popular front and of "boring from within."

The Czech *coup d'état* and the Berlin blockade preceded only by a short time the most dramatic and far-reaching disclosures that the House Un-American Activities Committee had ever heard in its long and staggering career. Beginning on July 30, 1948, Miss Bentley declared that throughout the 1930's and the war years, there had been Communists employed within the American government and that these Communists had committed espionage. On August 3rd Mr. Chambers asserted that eight high federal officials had been members of a spy ring. Persons as important as Mr. Harry D. White and Mr. Lauchlin Currie were mentioned as prominent figures in the network.

In those lax days when "classification" was either non-existent or was ridiculed by newcomers to the civil service as bureaucratic ceremonial, Soviet agents had apparently taken advantage of the Sovietophilia of a small number of Government employees, of their weak sense of organizational loyalty and their frivolous indifference to "security" requirements, and had obtained apparently quite considerable quantities of documents.[3]

Congressmen, journalists, some sober citizens and some who become excited by the thought of secrecy and clandestine goings on were not slow in making the connections. This was at a time when the secret of the atomic bomb still seemed to be the chief bastion of American security and when, by the aura which that secret spread onto other governmental activities, secrecy in general seemed absolutely important to the preservation of American life. The active

---

3. It is not known exactly what these documents contained. No consequences of significance in subsequent developments in international politics have, however, been traced to the collusion of American civil servants in Soviet espionage.

existence of the technique of "boring from within" inside
the United States Government was being demonstrated
against the background of the demonstrated effectiveness of
such a technique in Czechoslovakia.

Even quite imperturbable persons could have been legit-
imately dismayed by this juncture of events. Those who
incline towards anxiety and who are already disposed to
conceive of the world as a melodramatic struggle between
good and evil certainly found every ground for becoming
extremely agitated about the danger to America's secrets
arising from an internal conspiracy linked with the Soviet
capital of world conspiracy.

It should be recalled that until the postwar shock, the
American Congress had had no experience, even imaginary,
with conspiracy in the executive branch. Civil servants had
come in for some heavy blows in the second half of the
1930's and their opinions were sufficiently disliked for them
to be accused of disloyalty. Actual conspiracy had, however,
been beyond the limits of the Congressional imagination. It
had been the symbolic fact of disloyalty rather than real
dangers at which the Un-American Activities Committee
had bridled. The small minority of Congressmen who took
the Committee seriously were strong for publicity and homogeneity, but they had not reached the stage where secrecy
as such absorbed their attention.

The revelations of Miss Bentley and Mr. Chambers and
the Communist *coup d'état* in Czechoslovakia changed all
that. Conspiracy and disloyalty were very closely linked
thereafter.

VI. *The Insecurity of the Secret and*
Its Intractability

One of the reasons why there is so much disturbance
about the protection of secrets is that it is so extraordinarily
difficult to do it well. In the first place security policy, insofar as it is not merely physical security, is directed towards

the future. It is not a matter of putting a guard at a given place and preventing documents from being removed. It is rather a matter of entrusting documents to a person whose probability of disobeying the security rules must be estimated. The estimate must be made on the basis of very poor and fragmentary data of uncertain reliability[4] in accordance with principles of interpretation which are extraordinarily primitive at best, which have never been formulated and which perhaps can never be adequately formulated. Moreover, the standards of conduct to be avoided are vague and unstable. The confusion of loyalty and security-reliability adds to the unmanageability of the task.

This country has had little experience in this type of activity. No one knew for certain how serious the threat to security really was, and there were strong general tendencies to run to extreme reactions to the problem—either denying the significance altogether or elevating it into a problem of the most overwhelming significance. Not only did the ethos and experience of the country not provide guidance, but there was no professional tradition either. The rapidly expanding demand for security officers drew into the activity many men whose skill in detection might have been considerable, but whose skill in personnel assessment was less good.

One of the most needed qualities was a realistic understanding of the liberal and revolutionary traditions, their ramifications and the occasional points of contact. Practically no one in the Government possessed this knowledge, and the few such persons in and outside the Government were not attracted by nor considered for the post of security officer.

The situation was very little different in the recruitment of members for loyalty and personnel security boards. Although some quite distinguished men were drawn into this work, the understanding of the political currents of the

---

4. Members of the boards and security officers in many instances do not know anything of the reliability of the person who supplied the derogatory information to the field investigators.

1930's and of the diverse strands of radicalism of sentiment and doctrine has been largely lacking there too.

The danger of mistakes in dealing with problems which are indeterminate on their face but which could be terribly costly in their consequences has made for hardships and injustices for the victims and soul-searching uncertainties for those who have had to make the decisions.

The pressure of Congressional investigation and agitation has not aided in arriving at satisfactory solutions. It has, however, pushed decisions into the direction of greater strictness and suspicion. This was not so much because of fear of Congressional wrath, but because apprehensiveness was heightened by the increased prominence of the issue in the press.

The upshot of this inexperience and the intrinsic difficulty of the task has been that many current anxieties and deeper prejudices have found expression in decisions on particular individuals. That they have not done so all the time, and that Appeal Boards have often rectified the more alarmed and less balanced decisions of the lower boards, is evidence that numerous citizens kept their common sense about them in a situation uncomfortably new and requiring decisions about types of persons who have diverged rather widely from conventional American expectations.

CHAPTER 4

THE DEEPER SOURCES

I. *Hyperpatriotism*

THE POSTWAR DEVELOPMENTS centering about the Soviet Union have called forth such energetic and multiform responses because they touched on very sensitive nerves. Even a people as slow to respond to crises as the British have been moved to take protective action by the policy of the Soviet Union and its alliance with the Communist movement. In America, more excitable temperaments and a tradition of violence in expression and energy in action have prompted a passionate response to the threat of secret machinations.

The first and perhaps the most striking of the various elements in the traditional American outlook which underlies the agitation of the past decades is the American sense of nationality. Although the proportion of foreign-born persons in the United States had dwindled greatly in the past half-century, concern over the completeness of assimilation as a moral problem still remains strong. Being an American in relation to other Americans is not something which is taken simply for granted by virtue of residence in the United States in the way that being English, in relation to other Englishmen, is taken for granted in England. Except for refugees and expatriates, living in England defines one as English. In America, being American is not a primordial fact attendant on residence. In America, there is more of a tendency to define a person as American by the extent to which he acts and feels and thinks in a way defined as American.

The situation has been changing in the past quarter-century, and it is likely that without the stress arising from

immigration and political crisis, the conception of nationality as a matter of attitude and choice would have continued
to decline and would have become more a matter of long
residence. The crisis has, however, come upon a culture in
which the Americanization problem is still a real one for
many people, both consciously and unconsciously. People
remain aware of their differences *vis-à-vis* others in terms of
their attitudes towards America and often do not take for
granted the "Americanness" of their fellow countrymen.
There is more of a tendency in the United States, as compared with Great Britain, to think of differences in terms of
loyalty and disloyalty, in terms of liking and disliking America. Each successive tier of the nativity scale, each successive
generation of arrivals, looks askance on those who arrived
later or whose parentage is less completely American than
their own. Ethnic and nativity differences are reinterpreted
as attitudinal differences. The American way of life involves
the affirmation of ideals. Englishmen do not have to strive
to live an English way of life. Their way of life is English
by virtue of the fact that they live it. It is not quite the
same for those who speak so much about the American way
of life. They insist that an ideal be lived up to, that those
who would be American show it by their proclaimed beliefs.

It is natural for human beings who are uncertain of the
stability of their own conformity with a given standard to
abuse others for inadequate conformity with it. When men
are uncertain about the genuineness of their loyalties, they
tend to suspect others of not being genuine in their loyalties.
The United States is a country which has undergone rapid
changes; it is loose in its attachment to most traditions except those of individual freedom and reverence for the Constitution. Americans are relatively unbound by professional
and occupational ties and by local loyalties. When men's
loyalties are loosely anchored to particular places and institutions, they sometimes feel the need to be loyal more ur-
gently than do those persons and societies which are firmly
established in traditional loyalties. The very looseness of
loyalties, which on the one hand is a condition of freedom,

makes on the other hand for more sensitivity about loyalty. Periods of crisis make men feel the need for protection; they also make them need to feel loyal to some powerful protective institution such as a mighty national state. The less they are bound by professional and local loyalties, the more will they feel the need for the more inclusive loyalty and the more suspicious they will be of the genuineness and sufficiency of the loyalty of others.[1]

The combination of a state of mind which does not take its own national identity for granted with a general looseness of the ties which bind individuals to locality and corporate bodies, is conducive to an excessive recourse to the symbols of nationality when crises arise. Shocks which are not absorbed through the strength given by strong local and corporate attachments must be met by reaching out for the support of some other identification with a strengthening collectivity. In the United States, the reaffirmation of their national identity fortifies individuals, gives them a heightened sense of their own worth. It helps to establish them.

The tremendous expansion of American society and the rapidity of its development of new institutions means that movement upward in social position, in achievement and influence from the position of one's father is a rather common phenomenon. The American elites in business, politics, publicity and learning tend to come great geographical distances from the places of their birth to the places where they work and achieve. The great size of the country makes the loss of local ties in the leadership of the country a common phenomenon. Moreover, the cultures, the professional and social milieu into which the newly ascended leaders come, do not ordinarily possess powerful traditions which impose themselves firmly on most newcomers. There is no aristocratic or gentry pattern of life to which newcomers can clearly aspire and which they can definitely assimilate.

---

1. The weakness of the former type of loyalty will strengthen the disposition to think in terms of crisis, to interpret situations as if they were crises. Mobile, traditionless people will be quicker to see and proclaim a crisis than those whose professional and local loyalties hold them fast.

The American politician, to perhaps a greater extent than practitioners of other professions, realizes in his career the idea of the provincial boy of modest origins who takes advantage of the opportunities of an open society and rises to a high position in the national center. Even more than businessmen and intellectuals, successful American politicians have moved from the society of their birth and youth. They have moved from their earlier residences to Washington where they live away from their old friends and associates. They have given up their earlier occupation and they live in a world full of pitfalls and threats to their professional success. Many of them are, in the old term, "hyphenates" of fairly recent generations, and would like to live it down. The one firm foundation of their faith is therefore America, and all which threatens them is interpreted as a threat to America.

In consequence of this, we encounter, not infrequently among American politicians, an instant readiness to have recourse to their Americanism, to see differences between themselves and others as differences in degrees of adherence to American ideals and to the American way of life. They fall easily into the tendency to perceive their antagonists as disloyal to American standards.

The disposition towards hyperpatriotism is by no means confined to politicians in many of whom it is occasionally acute. What appears in the politician is simply a more severe form of popular hyperpatriotism rendered so by the more exposed position of the politician.

The suspicion of those whose ethnic or cultural traits appear to be insufficiently American has been a stable component of American provincial and small-town life for a long time. Lines of social status correspond to ethnic differences with the banker, the lawyer, the physician and the leading businessmen being the most American, the working classes the least American. Class antagonism was often expressed in and intensified by ethnic antagonism. In national crises when the nation seemed endangered, homogeneity in the "American way of life" was demanded. This demand rose in a great wave during the First World War, when Germans and even Scandinavians who have never been very productive of subversive activities in this country fell afoul of the hyperpatriotism of those whose zeal for assimilation had shot upward. In a number of states and municipalities, the foreign-speaking populations lost their newspapers and even their church services because laws and ordinances required that they hear, speak, and read only English. In the early 1920's the state governments, which had even less to fear from revolution instigated from abroad than the federal Government, busied theemselves in the pursuit of un-American influences. The Lusk Committee's Report is their chief literary monument. In the '30's state governments continued their search for un-American activities. What one finds in sharpened form among politicians, lawyers on the edge of politics, and dignitaries sufficiently worthy to be after-dinner speakers, one finds more diffusely but often more aggressively scattered throughout all classes of the population. Headed by those whose grip on their nationality should be firm enough not to require frequent and angry reaffirmation, i.e., the members of the societies of the older ethnic stocks, but whose hatred of foreigners equates them with subversives, the hyperpatriots draw their minority of support from all classes. When the threat comes from abroad, its subversive allies are found at home. The other way round, the pressure for Americanism at home and the contempt for the un-American heightens the belief in danger from abroad. What on the one side is hyperpatriotism, is, on the other, xenophobia.

II. Xenophobia

Xenophobia is no new feature of American life. It has appeared with varying strength ever since the outburst of Know-Nothingism against the Irish in the middle of the nineteenth century. Since that time, each recently arrived ethnic group has had a xenophobic streak in its bearing towards its successors on the lower levels of the social ladder. The Germans towards the Irish, the Irish towards the Germans who came later, both the Irish and the Germans and the older English and Scotch-Irish stock towards the South and East Europeans, the latter in their turn towards Mexicans and Puerto Ricans—and all together against the races and nationalities who have not had the good sense to come to this country.

Xenophobia, like hyperpatriotism, which is a vague effluvium in many quarters and a solid block of sentiment in a few, is the product of the extraordinary and perhaps unique success of the English-speaking elite in assimilating so many millions of persons of such diverse languages, cultures, and races. Xenophobia is the price paid for rapid and deeply penetrating assimilation. Asssimilation to American culture has necessitated a wrenching away from the older culture, but it did not usually succeed in a complete eradication of all traces of that culture. Assimilation required a strong, sometimes even stridently hyperpatriotic suppression of the earlier identity, and this was not always easy.

American xenophobia is a complicated affair. The product of a lingering attachment to what is still foreign, it is a violent denial of the value of being foreign. American xenophobia has taken the form of a hatred of the foreign coupled with a persisting attachment to the country of origin or extraction. The country's enemies are retained in this way and they are transformed into America's enemies. Thus an effective compromise with American patriotism is brought about.

The Irishman hates the British. The German-American retains some attachment to the land of his fathers and he jealously dislikes the British and despises the Poles and Italians; the Polish-American can still be aroused by the tribulations of his homeland and he is especially hostile towards the Russians and only a little less so towards the Germans; the Swedish-American loves to go back to Sweden to show off his superior Americanism, but also to be in the land from which his family came. Each feels some attachment to the old country and pays for it by being against foreigners in general, against foreigners in the United States and against the foreign connections necessitated by American foreign policy.

Xenophobia, hyper-Americanism, and attachment to the homeland have flowered into an even more complex pattern. One could be hyper-American and indirectly gratify one's attachment to the European homeland through Anglophobia.

England, which has been a home away from home for the American educated classes, both radical and conservative,[2] has been the touchstone of the un-American for the great mass of the American people in all classes. England with its social hierarchy, its elaborate etiquette of inequality, its symbolism of correct speech, the two-class railway system—which good Americans think has no counterpart in the United States—has been the *bête noire* of that rough-tongued but golden-hearted, outspoken, honest, shirtsleeved American, that good American of the frontier and populist traditions.

England came to be the genuine American's bad object for many reasons, gross and subtle. The prominence of the Irish in American political life gave a head start to Anglophobia. The resentment of Social Democratic German-Amer-

---

2. The radicals, if they are not revolutionaries, have admired England as the country where left-wing intellectuals can become really important as counsellors of governments and as public figures, free of harassment. The *New Statesman and Nation*—oddly enough— is greatly admired in the United States by sad little intellectuals who sigh in admiration and regret that America has no such organ. To these, the Fabian society seems one of the greatest achievements of the human spirit. It has been said with some justice that the late Harold Laski had more influence in America in the 1930's than he had in Britain—when the ideal developed of the left-wing, non-Communist intellectual, learned, elegant, witty, and fluent, and the intimate of Lords and trades unionists. The conservative American has admired in Great Britain the stately homes, the ancient colleges, the ascendancy of the well-bred over the vulgar, the beautiful silverware and furniture, the easy taking for granted of a rich inheritance.

In recent years, there has been a change. As the left intellectuals have become less radical and more anti-Communist, everything in England, in-including all their conservative compatriots once admired, has been engulfed in affection; neo-liberal American intellectuals have become critical of the state-controlled economy, the Welfare State and the supineness of the British businessmen in the embraces of the Welfare State.

icans against the then leading capitalist power in the world, the resentment of conservative German-Americans, thinking sentimentally of the Kaiser, against the great world power which rivaled and outshone Imperial Germany were both aggravated by the First World War and the unnecessarily harsh treatment which that war brought with it for German-Americans. The Poles, guided by Irish-American and German-American priests, hated the British for their Protestantism and their connection with the American upper class; the populistic, hard-working Scandinavian-Americans, both conservative and radical, were also antagonistic to the home of social hierarchy, of leisure, of scorn and condescension towards the lower classes, races and nationalities. Even the Jews, who had no foreign country to be attached to, were angry against the British for several decades because the British would not give them a foreign country of their own.

The resentment of the Middle Western farmer, bitter against the railways and banks controlled from the Eastern seaboard, of the pious fundamentalist farmer against the materialism of the metropolis (epitomized by New York), the bitterness of the Middle Western populist radical in city and country against the fortress of financial capitalism in New York—all drew an additional stimulus from the curious distrust of the links of friendship, marriage, financial interests and outlook on life which bound the wealth and culture of the Eastern seaboard to the British upper classes.[3]

The Anglophobia of the Middle and to a lesser extent the Far West, was a product of the will to be American and of the regional element in the American status hierarchy and class conflict. Middle Westerners, both rural and urban, were both in insurgency against the social and cultural preponderance of the wealthy and educated upper classes of the Eastern seaboard, and resentful of their predominantly British

---

3. Before the First World War, marriages between the plutocracy of the Eastern seaboard and the British aristocracy were quite frequent. Some British aristocratic families sought to replenish themselves from American wealth in a manner reminiscent of the way in which the British aristocracy had previously renewed and re-established itself by drawing into itself by marriage the daughters of the wealthy bourgeoisie.

origins and their British connections and sympathies. They resented their more refined speech, their more elaborate etiquette, their pretensions to social superiority and their economic hegemony. They resented their education, their sports and their leisure; they distrusted their whole style of life.[4] They disliked them for the yoke of culture and power which they imposed on the whole country and they disliked them for being so British in so many ways.

Within the United States Government, the State Department, more than any other part, was the habitat of the upper classes of the Eastern seaboard. Its quasi-British snobbery had always been the object of contempt and distrust, its gentility of manners brought it the accusations of being staffed by "cooky-pushers," "striped pants boys," and homosexuals.[5]

The State Department also drew the animosity of the American xenophobes from the very nature of the task assigned to it. Its task was to manage American foreign relations. The xenophobes did not like America to have foreign relations. Foreign states, especially the more powerful ones with whom relations were more noticeable, were regarded as archaic, cruel, undemocratic, deficient in sympathy for ordinary people and for small and weak nations. The xenopobes' conception of foreign policy was the avoidance of foreign relations, the encouragement of revolutions and the emancipation of subject nationalities.

The real fact of the matter was that the mass of the American middle class and much of the working class, especially in the Middle West, was fed up with old Europe, with its wars and its inequality. Not only were the foreign

---

4. Thorstein Veblen's whole life-work is a monument to this distrust of the polite, traditionally cultivated upper class founded on and maintained by mercantile, financial and industrial enterprise.

5. The class struggle between the lower and upper classes in this country has often taken the form of the denial of the manliness of the males of the upper classes. Being a "sissy," being named "Percy," etc., could happen to anyone, but it was thought that it was especially a feature of the boyhood and adolescence of the upper-class youth of the Eastern seaboard or of the restricted circles among the wealthy and respectable, who in other parts of the country sought to follow the Eastern model.

governments wicked and corrupt, but foreigners in general and in all classes had something wrong with them. They were not only old-fashioned, backward and lacking in ambition, but when they came to America they brought with them squalor and disorder. Their children became delinquents and criminals, they reproduced like rabbits, and they lived in filth.

The restriction of immigration in the early 1920's with its discrimination against Central, Southern, and Eastern Europeans was not just the result of the trade unions' desire to restrict the labor supply. It was powerfully reinforced in the working class and in all other classes by xenophobic sentiment. It was in part the aftermath and fulfillment of the desire to Americanize the immigrant population during and just after the First World War. It was part of the desire to break the connection with Europe.

III. Isolationism

Xenophobia, in addition to its diffuse hostility towards Europe in general and the more particular dislike of Great Britain, which epitomized the sins of old Europe, has had another, more specifically political manifestation. Xenophobia has lain at the root of the isolationism which raised its head after the First World War and which throughout the 1930's was an active force in American politics. In the Nye Investigations, in the Ludlow Amendment proposal, in the Neutrality Act, in the economic nationalism of the early Roosevelt years, isolationism showed itself in a variety of forms—pacifism, nationalism, populism, hostility towards the plutocracy with its European connections. Some of 'it was, of course, pro-German opinion among German-Americans still retaining some loyalty to Germany. Some of it came from anti-Semites and Nazis who were not numerous but who were very vigorous. Some of it, too, came from German-Americans who recalled with sadness the unhappy time for German-America which the hyperpatriotism of the First World War had brought with it. The Irish naturally contributed their share. But even among those who had some special interest in keeping the United States from concerning itself with Europe, their counsel of isolation was intermingled with the thought that America would do well to avoid being mixed up in the endless quarrels and animosities of a decadent and corrupt continent. Genuine idealism had a large share in this attitude. A sad, sighing shrug of hopelessness at the mention of Europe which started and tolerated wars and which, in fact, was so corrupted by the traditions of its ruling classes that it could never avoid them, was expressive of a widespread attitude. The general feeling was that it was best to have nothing to do with it.

It was difficult for America to overcome its isolationism. The prewar years induced a great strain in the United States. The desire to avoid the war, and above all to avoid entry into it once it had begun, generated an acrimonious debate. The debate mobilized all the residual impulses of American culture: Anglophilia and Anglophobia, hatred of Communism and friendliness towards socialism, anti-Semitism and hatred of cruelty and tyranny, bellicosity and pacifism, Xenophobia and idealistic internationalism, utopianism on a national and on an international scale, nostalgia for the faraway homeland and hyperpatriotism. The combinations of motives were many, but the country, or at least the politically interested sections of the population, gravitated towards two poles. The isolationists, who were strange bedfellows—democratic idealists, embittered opponents of President Roosevelt, pro-Nazis, Communists, Quakers, great patriots and psychopathic rogues—found that the situation forced a definition of the enemy. The enemy was the un-American intellectual, tied to the State Department and Franklin D. Roosevelt's administration. The enemy was the government which was moving towards intervention. After June 21, 1941, the Communists, who had never been welcomed into the isolationist camp, moved over to the interventionist side and the enemy was now further characterized by being pro-Communistic or under Communist influence.

It took the attack on Pearl Harbor and the Japanese,

German, and Italian declarations of war for Americans on
a grand scale to be willing to enter the battle. Even after
the war was well under way, the European war was repugnant to great numbers of Americans in the Middle West.
They felt that it was not "their" war. "Their" war was with
the Japanese who had attacked us. They felt there was a
justification for fighting the Japanese, but the European war
was only another dynastic quarrel among states which, if
no longer all monarchical, were still governed by old-fashioned ideas by which in the end they would encompass their
own ruin. Moreover, the pro-German element still hoped
that the Nazis would succeed in conquering Europe, if
America did not intervene there first. The first American
engagements were in the Pacific and General MacArthur
became a national hero, the thought of whose heroism slum-
bered in the popular bosom until it awoke with a roar in
the spring of 1951. Americans did not like either war, but
somehow the Pacific War seemed to be "our" war, while
the European war was the Europeans' war.

The decision to concentrate our first efforts in the European theater was not well received in the parts of the country
which had been isolationist. The dislike for that decision,
like the entry into the war in the first place, never died. It
went under the surface and took on a new form in the bitterness over the breakdown of Nationalist China before the
Communists. Thus isolationism, xenophobia, hyperpatriotism, and anti-Communism, which had been in quiet alliance
since the 1920's, joined in public and very vociferous alliance
against the State Department which had lost what General
MacArthur had gained or might have gained.

China had not been a great preoccupation of the American isolationists until after the war. The American interest in
China had been for a long time in the custody of the families
of missionaries and educators, and they had no political concerns other than a general love of China. The isolationists
adopted China only by the accident of the Pacific war having been the competitor of the European war, and by the
development of anti-Communism into a burning issue. Then

China provided a stick with which to beat the State Department. In 1950 when General MacArthur, the never-forgotten hero of isolationism, at a moment of great national exasperation about the Korean War and our initial reverses in it, seemed to offer a chance to defeat the Chinese Communists and even perhaps to bring the whole regime down and was not allowed to do so, isolationism with its commitment to the Pacific war and its reluctance about the European war flared up again.[6] It did not take the form of prewar isolationism and in fact it no longer stood for a policy of isolation and armed neutrality. It was now aggressively interventionist, but the sentiments and the fundamental pattern of thought remained as they had been before. The State Department was the major focus.[7] It had thrown away China while tying the United States to a European alliance which was immorally costly and by no means reliable. It allied us with Socialist and near-Communist nations; it counselled patience; it showed no capacity to resolve any difficult problems.

---

6. The North Korean invasion of South Korea served to whip up even more bitterness. Not only did the United States suffer the humiliation of the retreat from the Yalu River, but it fought the war with one hand tied behind it. This was especially infuriating to the ex-isolationists whose mind had become riveted on the Pacific and whose great hero, General MacArthur, protested against the restraints imposed on him by the Truman Administration.

The Korean crisis brought into focus many of the current grievances and worries. It gave the isolationists a cause, the Republicans another issue on which to attack the President and the Secretary of State, and it seemed to show that the connivance within the State Department which had brought the Communists to power in China was still favoring them by preventing General MacArthur from fighting against them with all the means at America's disposal.

Although he began his campaign some months earlier, it was during the long misery of the Korean War that Senator McCarthy made his greatest progress.

7. The Democratic Party as the party of European intervention and commitment, as the party which affronted the old virtues of self-reliance and individual initiative and responsibility, and which by its long tenure had infuriated the Republicans and made them desperate, shared with the State Department the burden of this renewal of isolationist passion.

IV. Fundamentalism

American society was severely shaken by the First World War. The theme of the old popular song "How're you going to keep 'em down on the farm, after they've seen Paree?" touched on a problem which after 1919 troubled the traditional morals of American society. America was a callow country before the First World War. It was still a puritanical country. The displacement of hundreds of thousands of rural and small-town youths as well as the young men of the big cities to Europe was an unsettling experience. Sexual ethics were disturbed by the novelty of multitudes of young men away from parental and communal control for the first time in their lives, in situations in which sexual promiscuity was tolerated and even encouraged by the cult of manliness common to large groups of youths just out of adolescence.

The depression and then the prosperity of the postwar years, the opportunities for new occupations, the great urbanization, and the self-conscious flaunting of conventional and legal standards in the consumption of alcohol, now rendered illegal by the Eighteenth Amendment, upset those who continued to live by the traditional morals. The "revolution in morals" was a motley thing: young women in bobbed hair; smoking cigarettes; the presentation before semi-popular audiences of ideas of sexual freedom and trial marriage—ideas which had previously been confined to narrow circles of "advanced thinkers"; the "scientific challenge" to orthodox Christianity, which by 1918 seemed to have yielded to the higher criticism and the theory of evolution; and in general a more hedonistic and frivolous attitude towards life. The vitality of the IWW and a general interest in the Russian Revolution among Eastern European immigrants and among intellectuals seemed to presage the growth of socialism with its denial of the right of a man to the fruits of his own labor and its rejection of the belief that every individual should be self-supporting. Religious faith and church attendance appeared to be on the decline. These changes offended the moral sentiments of rural and small-town people in the South and in the Middle West, where antipathy to the war still rankled.

This challenge to traditional morality aroused a variety of radical responses. An extremist, paranoid anti-Semitism developed a following in the Middle West. *The Dearborn Independent* with its phantasy of the Elders of Zion and their universal conspiratorial machinations was only the best known of a florid sprouting of anti-Semitic and anti-urban organs and conventicles. Anti-unionism and the fear of revolution also stirred throughout the country, especially in the business classes but also in other sections of the population. There was a harsh reaction against the rationalistic and latitudinarian tendencies in religious life, and fundamentalist strains of thought were revived. The Baptists and Presbyterians in the South and in the Middle West fought hard for orthodoxy, with support from Lutherans and Roman Catholics. This was all part of the reaffirmation of "old time religion."

In response to the "menace" of Bolshevism, state after state enacted criminal syndicalist and sedition laws and drastic, often violent action was taken against agitators and radicals. These activities were all parts of a larger effort to reaffirm and to re-establish the traditional pattern of society, not indeed so much to maintain the status quo, but to revive an idealized order which was alleged once to have existed.

On top of all this came prosperity. The country had never experienced such a rapid change in its standard of living. The new prosperity was accompanied by a great upsurge of hedonism. From callow virtue, America had swung towards pleasure. The traditional puritanical morals, both New England and Middle Western, Congregational and Lutheran, Baptist, Methodist, Irish Roman Catholic, Presbyterian and the myriad small Protestant sects which sprang from these were feeling the pressure of the new experience. The spread of more comfortable and luxurious modes of life tore men loose from traditional objects and traditional patterns of behavior. The scrapping of old styles and old furniture, the remodeling of houses, the introduction of the automobile, the casting away of the inherited material objects which embody memories and keep the past alive helped to cut American society away from its moorings.

The years between the end of the First World War and the beginning of the Great Depression were an offensive challenge to traditional morality on a grand scale. A puritanical, rigoristic morality, embittered, defensive, and suspicious against "foreign importations" was the response.

The prosperity of the late 1920's held the reaction in check, but in the meantime it was accumulating force. Guilt on the part of the beneficiaries and hatred on the part of the victims were the price of prosperity[8] which had to be paid when it collapsed. Then came the Great Depression which was a catastrophe, particularly for the rural population which still adhered to the traditional morality. Both the miseries and the relief of the 1930's were injuries to the traditional puritanical morality of the rural and recently rural population. As great a humiliation for the farmer as the loss of his farm was the need to depend on the government for support instead of relying on his own unaided efforts. Nor was it anything but galling to see other persons living from government payments and to know that in the cities men were being paid for "boondoggling." The Agricultural Adjustment Administration by its payment to farmers for producing less, for actually plowing up crops and destroying newly born animals, affronted the moral sense of the American farmers and of others too. It made them

8. A comment is in place on the influence of the unprecedented prosperity of the American people during the ten years following the Second World War. The increased prosperity, elevating people into new standards of living and into the perception of new possibilities, also led some of them to become more anxious about the future, to be troubled about a depression and about the precariousness of their possessions. The novelty of their new style of life made them more sensitive to the impingement of remote events; it made them more sensitive to questions of status; it increased their ideological receptivity.

Furthermore, the rag, tag and bobtail also became more aggressive and vociferous as a result of the increased prosperity. They felt more expansive and more powerful, and also more nervous; they felt more endangered by the twin dangers of subversion and espionage than if their lives were lived on a more even keel.

hostile towards the government and towards the civil service and the politicians who were parties to their moral degradation.[9] The Great Depression stirred many latent animosities and revived many ancient attachments in the American people. It generated a puritanical romanticism based on an ethic of "simple, virtuous individualism." It asserted the values of enthusiastic religion, of hard work and stern responsibility. It asserted the virtue of the small against the great, of the ordinary and the practical against the brilliant and the learned. The fundamentalist reaction of the 1930's was the protest of a rural society against the great society. It was a protest against the power of government as well as against the power of big business. It was the protest of tribalism against civility.[10]

Isolationism joined fundamentalism in hostility against the plutocrat during the depression years. The more internationalist one section of the population became, the more isolationist became another. The greater the readiness of the former to accept government assistance, the greater their satisfaction with governmental authority and intervention in economic life, the more hostile towards the actions of the government did the other, fundamentalist sector become. Ever since the 1920's American traditionalism, turned fundamentalist, fused with the neighboring streams of hyperpatriotism, xenophobia, and isolationism. In the 1930's they were joined by the torrent of populism which drew them into itself and which, in the intervening decades, has rushed forward with fluctuating but still mounting force, to batter at the sea wall of civility.

---

9. It was not difficult for the American farmer in the Middle West to believe that the Government consisted of persons of moral frivolousness, whose behavior is contrary to every moral law and whose vices consisted in seducing individuals into forgetting their moral responsibilities to themselves and to their families, and to dispense with the traditional moral standard of self-maintenance and self-sufficiency.

10. Fundamentalism in ethics and theology was part of a tribal ethic, not unlike Mau Mauism, produced from the traumatic impact of the crisis of civil society on those who have lost their place in the original tribal society and have not been able to come to terms with the civil society.

V. *The Fear of Revolution*

The United States has never had a substantial revolutionary movement. The IWW was perhaps the closest approximation, and its limited numbers, regional concentration and lack of immediate revolutionary intentions rendered it harmless. Nor has the United States even had a Socialist Party which paid lip service to revolutionary ideals while practicing moderation and social reform. There has been little enough in this country, apart from violence arising in connection with strikes, to frighten the propertied classes. Yet certainly since the 1880's major figures of the business community and a good number of their publicist associates have been studiously on the lookout for signs of revolution. Socialism and anarchism were the dangers warned against at the end of the century, when as far as America was concerned there were no such dangers. Then syndicalism was added to the list of dangers after the turn of the century. The Bolshevik revolution corresponded to the fears of the most hallucinated industrial plutocrats, corporation lawyers, and authors. From 1918 onward a small, loud, and aggressive collection of persons mainly in the business classes but scattered throughout the whole range of professions and occupations have seen Bolshevism or, as it is now called, Communism, as an ever-present threat to American society, to the American way and above all to the American system of private enterprise.

Throughout the country, before the rise to supremacy of the Federal Bureau of Investigation, many municipalities had "industrial" sections of their police force, and to these was assigned the protection of local industrialists from the menace of revolution. State police forces and legislative action were mobilized during the first five years following the end of the 1914-1918 war to prevent revolution. This meant occasionally preventing meetings from being held in small halls, raiding and sacking the local premises of the Socialist Party or the IWW or some fraternal foreign language association, and arresting trade union organizers, harrying subscribers to radical or liberal publications, collecting and acting on denunciatory gossip and so on. From time to time more drastic actions were taken. "Radicals" were run out of town, threatened and sometimes severely maltreated. Leaders of the IWW were tried and condemned to long prison terms, and even a mild socialist like Victor Berger was sentenced to twenty years' imprisonment. The Department of Justice outdid itself with raids and arrests on a grand scale.

So great and so unjustifiable was the disjunction between the magnitude of the threat which was meager and the magnitude of the response which was violent and powerful, that it is difficult to find a rational explanation. It cannot be explained simply by "class interests." There surely were some supporters of the repressive movement who saw in it an opportunty to forestall the unionization of their employees. On the whole, however, that could not explain the excitement and agitation which accompanied the harsh infringements on civil liberties after the First World War.

In venturing towards an explanation it is well to recall that in the imagery of the fear of revolution of those years the revolutionaries were almost always depicted as foreigners, unkempt, bearded, and named like Russians and Jews. Part of American extremist anti-revolutionism was the product of an exacerbated xenophobia, the xenophobia of the Northwest European-American stock against more recent arrivals from Eastern, Central and Southern Europe. There was probably a substantial component of anti-Semitism in it. It followed on the fierce wartime hatred of the "hyphenates." It was a carry-over of domestic hyper-Americanism whipped up by the war and class antagonism sharpened by the strikes of the immediate postwar period. Just as a quarter of a century later the atomic bomb aroused a great latent anxiety about secrecy, so the Bolshevik Revolution on a much smaller basis in reality aroused the animosities inherent in hyperpatriotism and the insecurities of class status.

Why should a sizeable fraction of American businessmen

have been so easily put off the path of hard-headed common sense, and why should politicians and high government officials have been stampeded into the unrealistic and unnecessary aggressiveness of the anti-revolutionary campaign of the early 1920's? Was it because American businessmen, hitherto unchallenged, were encountering the first challenges to their authority? They had withstood the populist and the muckraking attacks several decades earlier. Why did the post-1918 situation seem so much more dangerous? The earlier attacks had not involved the working classes as attackers in the same way. Working-class aggressiveness had been more occasional and scattered. The postwar strikes were on a larger scale. In addition to this, the aggressive working class was more "foreign" than it had been earlier. There were more "Bohunks," "Wops," "Polacks" and Ukrainians engaging in aggressive conflict now than earlier when the ethnic spread had not been so broad. It was more legitimate to be aggressive in return against persons of such disestimable ethnic origins. Further legitimation was provided by the occurrence of revolutions in some of the countries from which the foreign-born workers came. A direct link was imagined between the revolutions in Russia, Hungary, Austria, Germany and elsewhere in Europe and the aggressive class struggle conducted in the United States by persons born in these countries. The fact that the European revolutionary movements were followed with such interest by small groups of immigrants in America made the anti-revolutionaries sure that a revolution was being plotted in the United States through secret links with the foreign centers of revolution.

In the latter half of the 1920's, anti-revolutionary anxieties were calmed and gave way before a rather boorish illiberality of mind. The Great Depression, however, unsettled this calm. First businessmen were degraded, menaced by the failure of their enterprises and reduced in public esteem. They were charged with the responsibility for the economic crisis. Then when the Government began to take measures to relieve distress, it did so mainly by methods alien to the experience of businessmen and indeed often coupled with assaults against the dignity of private entrepreneurial activity. This was painful for businessmen, and as they gradually recovered their self-esteem (they did not do so fully until the 1940's), they began to attack the system which they feared was replacing them. Digging into their store of prejudices inherited from earlier decades, they found the twin menaces of socialism and communism. (The anti-revolutionary extremists practically never distinguish between socialism and communism.) The extension of government activity and rule by bureaucrat-intellectuals was too much for their traditional outlook. Businessmen had been used to ruling the roost in their communities, above all, outside the great metropolitan centers. The new power of the federal government and the exercise of that power by university teachers, professional social scientists and lawyers from Harvard and Columbia University Law Schools was decidedly unpleasant.

Leadership in the life of most American communities is provided not by a landed gentry attended by its solicitors and professional devotees; it is in the hands of the businessmen who provide much of the effective civic and political leadership and who dominate, in collaboration with professional men, the culture of the town. Their culture is a man's culture and a business culture. It is manly and aggressive. It is a culture which is not extremely deferential towards intellectuals, towards literary men and university and college teachers. The businessmen's culture has its own ideals of civil life. In those ideals, the major role is played by businessmen.

They are not anarchists, but they do not like government particularly. Many of their best friends are in politics, but they do not spontaneously and enjoyably think of politics as central to the life of the country. There have been great changes, and they know that the world is not what it was. Nonetheless, their picture of the ideal world has, in the main, been a world without politicians and especially one without bureaucrats intervening in economic life and molesting and constraining businessmen.

Accordingly, when in the 1940's intellectuals, civil servants, spies and atomic secrets were tangled together by the juncture of events, businessmen, once more restored to their earlier dignities and still not at ease, produced many fervent supporters for the battle against conspiracies instigated by foreign enemies.

VI. Populism

Populism proclaims that the will of the people as such is supreme over every other standard, over the standards of traditional institutions, over the autonomy of institutions and over the will of other strata. Populism identifies the will of the people with justice and morality.

American populism survives in our minds as a type of progressive rural radicalism. It has left behind memories of great humanitarians like Norris and LaFollette and of idealistic reformers who in a great society sought to give power back to the people—through the referendum, the initiative and the recall, through control of the railroads and the public utilities, etc. But populism has many faces. Nazi dictatorship had markedly populistic features in its practice, in its constant invocation of the will of the people as its justification and the good of the people as its end, and in the "direct" relationship of the people and their leader unmediated by institutions. Bolshevism has a strand of populism in it too, although, like National Socialism and other dictatorships, its practice rejects the will of the people as a guide; nonetheless, in Bolshevism too the praise, however spurious, of the people continues an older tradition of belief in their superior wisdom and virtue. Populism is not confined to the "left" and it is not confined to the lower classes. It can enter into the outlook of governing classes, into the professions, into strata which do not from their own interior life produce a populistic outlook. In the United States, populism lives on in persecutory legislative investigations, in the security-loyalty policy of the federal Government and in the loyalty policies of the lesser bodies. McCarthy is the heir of LaFollette.

What was populism if not the distrust of the effete East and its agents in the urban Middle West? Was not populism the forerunner of "grass roots" democracy? Did it not seek to subject the Government to the people's will, to tumble the mighty from their high seats, to turn legislators into registrants of the people's will? Was it not suspicious of the upper classes of the East? Did it not seek a world free from the constricting entanglements of the Old World, with its hierarchical pretenses and its dynastic ambitions? Was not populism "folksy," quick to use Christian names, hail-fellow-well-met, in contrast with the cold, inhuman impersonality of upper-class etiquette? Did not populism speak about the "interests," the "cliques," "caucuses," "lobbies" and "rings" which held the people in chains, depriving them of the fruit of their labors? Did not populism allege to protect the people and their government from conspiracies, from cells of conspirators who, contrary to the people's will and through the complacency or collusion of their rulers, were enabled to gain control of society? Does not populism deny the right of privacy on behalf of publicity and does it not do so to protect the people from conspiratorial secrecy?

Populism is distrustful of the "overeducated." The great state universities which the Middle West has created were intended to provide education and learning which would be different from the arid refinements, useless subtleties, and the leisured snobbery of Harvard, Yale and Princeton. They were intended to reach a different class of students, to provide them with something different from what the universities of the East were doing. They were intended to produce hard-headed, tough-minded citizens, capable of keeping their government in their own hands, and technicians and civil servants of popular government. The higher reaches of pure science and scholarship, in which some of the Middle Western state universities have taken a great place, were not the first responsibilities of those universities.[11]

When populism goes on the warpath, among those they wish to strike are the "overeducated," those who are "too clever," "the highbrows," the "longhairs," the "eggheads," whose education has led them away from the simple wisdom and virtue of the people. Progressive populism did not hesitate to intrude into the internal affairs of its universities, and loyalist populism in its fear of secrecy still does not hesitate to do so. It is not difficult to see in Senator McCarthy's fulminations against Harvard, that "sheltered sanctuary" of the Fifth Amendment of the Constitution of the United States, the "grass roots" prophet assailing the aristocratic battlements of pure learning which have despised the wisdom of the people. From the perpetual harassment of the local schoolteacher in the small town to the enthusiasm of the state legislatures in enquiring into subversion in the educational system, to the grand passions of the Congressional committee investigating subversion and conspiracy in the universities and private foundations, the resentment against the learned person who is not "one of the boys" is at work. Populists, whether they are radical reformers or congressional investigators pursuing weak links in security, are all extremely suspicious and hostile towards the more sophisticated person, who, they think, stands apart and does not share what is on his mind with the likes of them, who thinks he is better than they are, and secretly might be thinking of subverting them. All the recent preoccupation with those who withhold themselves in enclaves differentiated from the rest of the society reveals more than a trace of populistic hostility towards those whose learning has drawn them away from the common life.

Populism, although it is known historically as a primarily Middle Western and Southern phenomenon, is a much more widespread phenomenon. It exists wherever there is an ideology of popular resentment against the order imposed

---

11. The achievements of pure science and scholarship in the state universities is evidence that the populistic conception of the university has not dominated the universities completely or destroyed their autonomous powers.

on society by a long-established, differentiated ruling class, which is believed to have a monopoly of power, property, breeding and culture. The Middle West and, to a lesser extent, the South, where the populace was coming into political self-consciousness and the ruling class was not near enough at hand to impose its culture through immediate personal relationships, but powerful enough at a distance to make its political and economic power felt, were the proper birthplaces of American populism. In the South, an older aristocratic ruling class lay in ruins without property or power; its economic and political feebleness and pretensions to breeding and culture were a fertile ground for populistic denunciation of the upper classes. The Middle West, feeling deprived by an Eastern and ethnically alien ruling class, was even more fertile ground. Both regions possessed resentfully aggressive classes who provided the motive force for populism.

Populism, by its tendency as an organized political movement and more so by the permeative tradition which it has injected into an already favorably predisposed egalitarianism, has brought about a peculiar inequality. Originally a protest against the wealthy and great, in their splendor and state, it inclines easily by the radicalism of its emphasis towards an inverted inegalitarianism. Populism is tinged by the belief that the people are not just the equal of their rulers; they are actually better than their rulers and better than the classes—the urban middle classes—associated with the ruling powers.

The mere fact of popular preference is therefore regarded as all-determining. Emanation from the people confers validity on a policy and on the values underlying it. Populism does not deny ethical standards of objective validity, but it discovers them in the preferences of the people. The belief in the intrinsic and immediate validity of the popular will has direct implications for the rule of law. It denies any degree of autonomy to the legislative branch of government, just as it denies autonomy to any institutions. Demanding that all institutions be permeated by the popular will or responsive to it—since the validity of the popular will is self-evident—populism inclines towards a conception of the legislative branch which may be designated as "identity" in contrast with "representation." Legislators are expected to be "identical" with the popular will rather than "representatives" who will interpret it. Populism is impatient of institutional traditions and boundaries; it finds the delimitation of jurisdictions so much "bureaucratic red tape" which strangles the popular will. It is impatient of institutional procedures which impede the direct expression of the popular will and the forceful personalities who assume the responsibility of being vessels of the popular will. Populism is impatient of distinctions and it abhors the division of powers which would restrain and confine the popular will. Populism is blind to the possibility of the impartial and disinterested performance of duty. It hates the civil service, which it regards as an obstacle to substantive justice, but also because it believes that everything is "political." From Andrew Jackson to Mr. Scott McLeod, populists have been convinced that civil servants cannot be trusted to carry out the orders of their political superiors unless they are imbued with the beliefs of their superiors.[12]

Populism seeks substantive justice. It cares not at all for the traditional rules in spheres of life outside its own immediate sphere. It regards the legal system as a snare for the guileless, a system of outdoor relief for lawyers and judges; it regards administration as a morass for the entrapment of the unwary and the virtuous. It regards politicians as artful dodgers, as evaders of responsibility, as twisters with fine words but ready to compromise away the interests of those for whom they stand. It regards the monetary system and the banks as a vast system of traps for depriving the poor of what they are entitled to and for enriching idlers.

Populism—not just populism in the specific historical

12. Mr. McLeod recently said, "In the second, third, and fourth echelon of employees, the policy which originates at the top must be implemented. Until such time when we can re-educate those employees or replace them with proper personnel, the progress which we make is sometimes very slow."

meaning, although that was an instance of the species—regards parliamentary politicians as very inferior beings with no inherent virtue in themselves or in their institution. Politicians are at best errand boys with little right to judgment on their own behalf if that judgment seems to contradict popular sentiment. The administrative branch is even less exalted—discolored as it is by corruption and indolence at an earlier date and excessive education and looking-down on the ordinary people in latter days. The derogatory attitude towards the politician described above, which originated in quite a different moral climate, articulated perfectly with the populist view. But, even without that reinforcement, populism in all countries—even in countries with memories of aristocratic ruling classes, e.g., Germany—is hostile to the politician.

Populism is not, however, recalcitrant to leadership. Great spellbinders who would bring populists substantive justice are capable of moving them and of bending them to their will. Middle Western populism produced its great men, like LaFollette and Norris—morally serious men whose genuine concern for the poor and whose aversion for great inequality in wealth, power and status, endeared them to their grave and sober German-American and Scandinavian-American constituencies—and like Bryan, the great spellbinder who fought the war of the country against the city, of the plain man against the banker, who stood for simple rectitude and orthodox religion and whose later role in the fundamentalist struggle against secularism was part of the broader pattern of populism. The areas which produced the populism of the end of the nineteenth century and the early twentieth century have continued to produce them. There is a straight line from Ben Tillman to Huey Long and Eugene Talmadge; from Bryan and LaFollette to Gerald L. K. Smith, Father Coughlin and Senator McCarthy, Gerald Nye, William Langer and many others.[13]

---

13. Populism is not just a rural phenomenon. It is urban as well. It appears in a modified form in revolutionary parties and under constraint in the big city political machine. It appears wherever people want "help and

Populism acclaims the demagogue who, breaking through the formalistic barriers erected by lawyers, pedants and bureaucrats, renews the righteousness of government and society. Populism is impatient of checks and balances, it is restive under the restraints imposed by the separation of powers. Senator McCarthy's appeal to subordinate employees of the executive branch to bring to him whatever they deem relevant to the security of the country from the Communist conspiracy is characteristically populist in its disregard for the boundaries of institutions and for the niceties of institutional responsibilities. The detailed control of the policy of an executive agency, through the threat and actuality of investigations or through forcing the appointment of particular individuals to key posts, such as the Senate Subcommittee on Government Investigations attempted to exercise over the Voice of America and the United States Information Service, or which the appointment of Mr. McLeod has rendered possible in the State Department, seems right and proper from the populist point of view. The legislator is the agent of the people's will and it is his obligation to make that will prevail everywhere and immediately. There is no division of responsibilities which is legitimate to the populist.

The populistic conception of the politician affects not only the expectations held by the populace regarding the politicians' behavior. It also affects the politician's own conception of his obligations.

---

not justice," where they seek the redress of their wrongs through the direct intervention of powerful personalities and not through the endless labyrinth of legal institutions.

CHAPTER 5

THE STRAIN OF POLITICS

I. The Situation of the Legislator

IN THE UNITED STATES, as in any other large democratic government, the burden on the legislator is great. The volume of legislation is vast and its complexity beyond the judgment of laymen. Even an expert could not hope to understand and master fully all the bills which are produced. In Great Britain, where the party leadership strictly controls the introduction of legislation and private members' bills are the exceptions, the detailed mastery of all proposed legislation is beyond the power of all Members of Parliament. In the United States, where so many nearly similar bills are produced on the same subject, where the number of subjects on which legislation is proposed is vast, and where individual legislators often have their own legislative ambitions in addition to the program of their party leaders and of the Executive, the burden is especially great. The legislator is overwhelmed by his legislative work alone. He frequently votes on measures on which he has not formed his own judgment and on which he has not had his judgment authoritatively and reassuringly formed for him by his party organization. The fact that he leaves so much uncovered has a disquieting effect on him; it causes him to feel that matters are slipping beyond his control. The American legislator does not inherit a tradition of a political class who have a sense of having been born to rule. American legislators come from a great diversity of backgrounds, but for a long time they have come from moderate provincial circumstances in which there was no sense of a natural affinity to authority. The self-esteem of a traditional political class has been lacking in the tradition of American politics, and the effects of the absence have been aggravated by the prestige of the "people."

The discipline of the British parliamentary party and the power of the national headquarters lightens the burden of judgment and worry for the British M.P. If he behaves himself reasonably well, he can count on the support of his party for re-election. The decentralized structure of the American party system and absence of disciplinary power of the party leadership in Congress accentuate, on the contrary, the strains on the American legislator. He is very much on his own. The national party does not arrange his candidacy; it has little control over the machine on which the Congressman depends for his re-election; and its financial aid for the conduct of his campaign is much less than adequate. He must keep his machine going. Like an ambassador who is uneasy that his enemies at home are undoing his work and undermining his position while he is away, the legislator must always keep his eye on the machine at home—fearing that it might break out of his control during his absence in Washington.

American constituents, at least a sector of them, are often very outspoken in their demands. The American legislator is moreover hypersensitive to the faintest whisper of a constituent's voice. Unable to depend on the national party for re-election, he must cultivate and nurture the more active elements in his constituency more than legislators in Great Britain where constituents are less clamorous and parties are stronger at the center.

To satisfy the demands of some of his constituents the American legislator expends much of his time and energy running errands for them in Washington and receiving them when they visit the capital for business or for sightseeing purposes. He himself is often quite pleased to have this opportunity for personal contact with his constituents, even though it distracts him from his job in Washington.

In addition to trying to please those whom he sees, he is constantly harried in his mind's eye by those whom he does not see. His remoteness from them does not make him less sensitive to their sentiments or less fearful of their displeasure. The distance from the voters and their anonymity make the sensitivity even greater and more delicate. The nature of the recruitment process favors the man with a delicate ear for the voters' sentiments and an eagerness to gain their approbation. The populistic ethos of the American electorate and the traditions of American politics favor the person who can present himself as a man of the people, who is proud of the fact that he deviates from them in no significant way and who fears that any known deviations would be interpreted as snobbery or stand-offishness.

This eagerness to gratify an unseen constituency and to rank high in their favor helps us to understand why it is that legislators who have no strong convictions on a given topic might sometimes be among its most fervent investigators. They do so simply because they believe it will appeal to their constituents and because they cannot allow any rival for the affection and votes of their constituents to pre-empt this theme.

Far from his home base and insecure about his tenure and support, he is hard put to find a procedure for keeping in touch with his constituents and fixing himself in their minds. The press conference, the cultivation of newspapermen, the radio and the television program, and the congressional investigation are often the best-suited instruments for the legislator's need to remind his constituents of his existence. That is the reason why investigations often involve such unseemly uses of the organs of publicity. By giving material to the press, he pleases the journalists and reaches the eyes of his constituents. Publicity is the next best thing to the personal contact which the legislator must forego. It is his substitute offering by which he tries to counteract the personal contact which his rivals at home have with his constituents.

The frequent recourse to personal intervention on behalf of individual constituents has greater consequences than the maintenance of a sensitive attachment of the legislator to his audible constituency and the wasteful expenditure of his time. It encourages in him expectation of personal service by the bureaucracy, an expectation long entrenched in the traditions of patronage politics and populism.

The American legislator, whose professional traditions date back to a social order in which government intervention played no great part and in which patronage was the main method of the recruitment of civil servants, tends to look on the administrator's role and tasks as properly the legislator's own responsibility—which are only transiently delegated to the administrator. He draws no fine line between legislation and administration and he likes to co-operate in and assist in administration as well as to specify, scrutinize, and control the administrator's tasks and powers. The modern separation of powers is indeed often felt as an implicit rebuff.

To these particular strains in the vocational life of an American legislator should be added the more general strains. For one thing, the career of the professional politician is full of hazards. In all democracies the legislator is recurrently in danger of not being re-elected. In the event of being unsuccessful he must go back to a career which he has neglected. In the United States very few of our professional politicians are recruited from the classes which live from inherited wealth. If he is in the professions or business, he will, if defeated for re-election, have to make up the distance which his contemporaries have gained on him. Although he might have improved certain "connections," some of his skill other than political skill might well have deteriorated. He will probably have allowed some of his professional connections to lapse. Whatever the effect on his skill he often faces the humiliation of return as a political failure, and the need to begin at a lower level than those who were his equals a few years before. Moreover, since our politicians do not come from classes which have as part of their tradition a normal expectation of entering a political career, they tend to a greater extent to be selected from among persons who enjoy the game of politics, to whom it has a special psychological appeal. For such persons, the threat of exclusion from politics through failure is especially unsatisfactory. Thus the situation of the political career in the United States makes legislators faced with the possibility of failure take eager refuge in devices which will recommend them to their constituents and reassure their continuation in office. Activity as a member of an investigative committee bathed in publicity is one of these devices.

Even when successful, however, the professional politician in the United States cannot always have the unalloyed pleasure and comfort of feeling that he is participating in a highly honored profession. The fact that he is so often made into an errand boy or a handmaiden to his constituents is indicative of their attitude towards him and of his attitude towards himself. Government in the United States, where established institutions are not usually objects of deep reverence, is far from the most esteemed of institutions. Living from the public treasury, from the taxpayer's money, whether as legislator or administrator, has until recently been rather looked down upon by the hard-working taxpayer and his journalistic spokesmen. This view is still alive in American public opinion. The image of the politician in the organs of mass communication is not a laudatory one. Pomposity, vanity, an unbalanced sense of importance and occasionally sheer dishonesty are part of the traditional American concept of the professional politician—although the reality has been far different. Even though this popular image has been changing in the past decades, the term "politician" still has a derogatory overtone.

It is significant that there is no word in current usage to describe the legislator which is free from either cant or derogation. The word "politician" in the United States brings a wrinkle—and scarcely a smiling one—to the nose. There is no other word save "statesman" for the job, and it always evokes uneasiness and visions of diplomatic chancelleries and of elegant gentlemen who have a rather hard time at the hands of the politicians. The fact that the United States is simultaneously the freest of great states and at the same time the scene of some of the most unworthy departures from the principles of liberty and the rule of law is closely connected with the devaluation of the politician in American life.

The occasional outbursts of an excessive desire to please on the one hand, and of vindictive aggressiveness on the other, are both products of this perception by the professional politician of his ambiguous status. The legislator's suspicion of the administrator as one who lives wastefully on the taxpayer's money is also an expression of the discomfiture which arises from the uneasy feeling that he himself is doing exactly that. Congressional investigations often provide favorable occasions for the manifestations of this deep-lying distrust.

It is not only the social status of politics that influences the legislator's mood. The geographical location of the center of national political life also has its effect. The almost exclusive position of politics as the chief preoccupation of Washington has an influence on the life of the legislator. It means that he is forced to live almost entirely in an atmosphere of politics. It is true, of course, that many enjoy this type of life with its incessant stress on influence, rivalry, ambition and frustration—it sharpens political wits and has a brilliance of its own. It does, however, strengthen and even overdevelop the political orientation of men who have already entered voluntarily upon such a career. It aggravates the exclusive preoccupation with political events to the point where every human activity becomes evaluated not in terms of its intrinsic value in its own appropriate sphere, but in terms of its political significance.

In London, a legislator can carry on his own profession if he is fortunate, which is more frequently the case than in Washington. He can also associate more easily with persons in other professions, with businessmen, scientists, writers, clergymen, in fact with all the groups which the diversified life of a great city which is not merely the political and administrative capital of a great country makes possible. A diversity of interests and a reduction of the primacy of politics is more practicable in this kind of situation.

In Washington, however, legislators must associate in their leisure hours almost entirely with other legislators or with journalists, administrators, and businessmen whose presence in Washington is almost always evidence of their own predominantly political interests. In such a society, where the talk is invariably centered about who is getting what from whom, both the sensitivity and the insecurity of the legislator are increased. It strengthens his tendency to interpret everything in political terms and to look on the world as engaged at every moment in arranging political combinations, intended to advance some individual or group and to ruin another. This type of social life offers no respite from the tensions and anxieties of the individual legislator's own political career. It provides a stimulant rather than a soothing calm. The gossip and rumors agitate him and cause him to worry more about his own political fortunes. Hearing so much of what others are doing or are having done for them to secure their political fortunes, he feels he must exert himself more to establish and advance his own prestige. Whoever blocks him is his enemy. Whoever has a deficiency, real or imputable, which can be attacked in the name of a major political value, becomes a fair target in the competition to keep oneself politically afloat. He is more susceptible to excitation by rumors and by the passing currents of opinion.

As a result of these factors—not all of which operate equally for all legislators—the life of the American politician holding a seat in the Senate or in the House of Representatives is far from an easy one. He is always confronted with more demands on him than he can satisfy. He is always in danger of displeasing some people and he is never sure of just what it will take to please them or how he can do it when he knows what it is. He is always dependent on someone else's judgment for his equanimity and for his security, and he tends to be a person with a desire to please. The result is a state of stress and disquiet, often flaring up into rage and sometimes into vindictiveness.

If we bear in mind the populistic atmosphere in which

the political career is conducted, and the populistic dispositions which many of our political leaders carry with them as a product of their own spontaneous outlook and as a product of the need to read and please their constituents' minds, we begin to understand why political life in the United States is often so stormy, and why so many politicians seek their salvation in publicity. We also begin to see why politicians have conspiracies on their minds and why they are preoccupied with secrecy.

A closer examination of the politician's relations with administrators and intellectuals will show how the fears and anxieties of politicians have come to a head in our recent disturbance about conspiracy and secrecy.

II. Politician vs. Bureaucrat

The traditions of the American Congress and the outlook of our Congressmen are the products of a free society in which it was neither necessary nor desirable that large powers be assigned to the executive branch of the government. The inevitability of the assignment of great powers to the executive under modern conditions is often intellectually acknowledged by our legislators, but there is also resentment against this necessity and, more deeply, an unwillingness to accept it. The continuing necessity for large-scale governmental activity in this country during the past twenty-five years, through the depression, the war and the postwar period of incessant tension, has created an immense bureaucracy. The bureaucracy has been on the whole energetic, capable, and intelligent, full of ideas and projects and not too pleased to see their plans curbed by an unsympathetic Congress.

The administrator is regarded as the usurping rival of the legislator, and sometimes as an actual obstruction to the realization of the people's will. General laws, when implemented in detail by administrators, often work hardships on particular constituents. The legislator is often unable to persuade the administrator to remove that hardship. In many cases the derogation of his power and status which this implies is unhappily felt by the legislator, and animosity against particular administrators and against the executive branch and bureaucracy in general is fostered.

This attitude is also affected by the diminution of the patronage system in the recruitment of federal civil servants. A civil servant appointed by patronage is the creature of the legislator. Patronage remains one facet of American politics despite the establishment of the merit system in the federal civil service. The important role in the national parties of local and state "machines," subsisting on patronage, is responsible for this. A legislator who has passed through the lower levels of the party on his way upward tends to expect civil servants to respond to him as though they are personally beholden to him. The fact that this is not so is very evident to the ordinary administrator and it is manifested in his behavior.

The contact between legislators and administrators who appear before the various standing committees and special committees is often frustrating to the legislator. There is seldom a direct challenge to the status of the legislator, but the authoritative and self-assured way in which the administrator disposes of his own knowledge and the legislator's questions can also become a source of uneasiness. The administrator, as an expert, deals self-confidently with a matter which the legislator does not always grasp with the same measure of self-confidence. When the subject matter of the hearings is one about which the legislator already has grievances, the result is apt to be a further rankling of his sentiments. The resulting "soreness" occasionally reveals itself in the support and conduct of investigations directed against the particular administrator, and against the executive branch and bureaucrats in general.

This particular friction is, in part, one of the by-products of the merit system. The civil servant, particularly the civil servant of the level called before Congressional committees, will often be more educated and his social and economic origin will probably be higher than the legislator's, who is requesting a service of him or interrogating him. He is not only more expert in the matter at hand, but he usually, either wittingly or unwittingly, is also more the master of the situation than the legislator. Resentment against those whose fortunate accidents of birth gave them educational opportunities which were not available to the legislator is sometimes heightened—it certainly was heightened during the Roosevelt administration—by an attitude of personal, social and intellectual superiority on the part of the administrator. This sense of superiority very often does not exist at all, but is nonetheless often assumed to exist and is as bitterly resented as if it were real.

The persistent rise in the educational level of the civil service and the delegation of vast legislative powers to a resourceful and ingenious executive has only reinforced a difficulty which is endemic in the American constitutional system, namely, the thorough separation of the legislative and executive branches. That the President to some extent and, even more, his cabinet members (except generally the relatively insignificant Postmaster General) are often new to Washington politics and cannot usually be regarded as "one of the boys" deepens the breach between the legislators and the executive branch. It increases the likelihood of misunderstandings which accumulate and which cannot easily be cleared up by informal personal interchange or prevented by the existence of close personal relations or friendship. The fact that the President's advisors are usually neither professional politicians nor civil servants of long standing with a seasoned intimacy with the ins and outs of Washington political society makes for a breach at the top.

Some of these frictions are in the nature of our constitutional situation. If legislators are intended to watch over the execution of the laws they pass and to scrutinize the laws recommended to them by the executive branch, some friction will necessarily exist. It is, however, exaggerated by the adventitious element of the legislator's representation of the private interests of particular constituents. It is also driven further by the fact that except for personal intercessions and questioning in committees, the American legislator has no control over what he regards as injustices or inefficiencies in the working of the administrative system. He must intervene personally, often at the cost of much time and energy, or he must attempt to hold up the appropriation for an entire section of the administration. If he fails in the first, and the second alternative is not available to him, only the investigative committee remains. It is certainly not always easy to start such a committee, and a long accumulation of hurts and grievances will usually have been felt before the committee can be created and got under way. He must wait until enough other legislators think the issue is a good one or until, for some other reason, enough other legislators are willing to allow him to go ahead. The long period of waiting and the gradual fusion of resentments from a great variety of sources make it more likely that the investigation will be rough. Even if he is not on the committee himself, he will often support it because it is a vicarious way of soothing the many frustrations he has experienced at the hands of bureaucrats.

There is little opportunity for the release of pressure by moderate means, such as the question period in the House of Commons, which provides a regular opportunity for the airing of small injustices and prevents an accumulation first of personal animosity and second of animosity in general. The possibility of having a particular wrong corrected imposes a sense of responsibility on the person who is trying to bring about the correction. If the situation has been allowed to go so far that accusations are generalized and no immediate corrections expected—when the legislator feels that he is shouting into the wind—then his accusations will become louder and angrier and his wrath will be less easily and effectively appeased. Yet this is the atmosphere in which investigations into the doings of the executive branch are too often launched.

The conflict between Congress and the civil service, which up to a point is a requirement implicit in the Constitution and fundamental to the needs of a democracy for protection against an imperious and insolent officialdom, has been exacerbated by the policies which bureaucrats have created and executed. A partially autonomous bureaucracy, independent of Congressional patronage, more expert and in some ways of a higher social status, would be irritating enough to politicians working under these strains. But beyond this, the policies enacted by the legislators and executed by the civil servants have often run against some of the moral sentiments of the legislators, even those who helped bring them into law. Only a minority among our legislators were enthusiastic for the social security legislation and the economic policies of the prewar Roosevelt administration. Their fears of subversion were made more plausible to them when they saw civil servants carrying out policies which seemed to them so socialistic. Projects like the raking of leaves in public parks, the provision of subsidized housing, payments to farmers for keeping acreage out of cultivation, the protection of the right of membership in trade unions, the organization of Greenbelt communities—all of these and many others seemed in the 1930's to many legislators of old-fashioned backgrounds to be contrary to the principles of private enterprise. Even though a great number of Congressmen are hostile to big business, they prize the competition of private enterprises run by self-made men whose workmen are paid only for what they do and not what trade union monopolies charge. The policies were contrary to their ethical views regarding the relations between work and reward and their ideas of individual responsibility. They were not enthusiastic about the policy of aid to Great Britain, and even less so about aid to the Soviet Union. They have not been enthusiastic about the Marshall Plan or about military aid to Europe and now to Southeast Asia. They have been forced by their own intelligence and sense of responsibility to do what they would have preferred not to do; and they were forced by what they thought was public opinion, by powerful popular Presidents like Roosevelt and Eisenhower, or by a President whom they did not like but who was able to point to the menace of Soviet Communism.

If they had to yield on policies, then they sought to recoup their self-esteem by harsh scrutiny of the execution of the policies. It is not a far cry for those who regard their own image of the proper economic and ethical system as an integral part of the hyperpatriotic ideal to conceive that whatever deviates from this image or attacks it to be part and parcel of the Communist effort at subversion.

The strains which arise from our constitutional system, our cultural background and the substance of governmental policy are aggravated during periods of strong executive leadership and the expansion of the executive powers. Strong executive leadership appears, while it is working, to cure the ailment, but under our present conditions it nonetheless leads to aggravation.

The dry fruit of this aggravation is harvested in the period of weakest leadership. Jealous though they are of their powers and prerogatives, legislators normally renounce some of them during periods of national crisis. This was what happened under the administration of Franklin Roosevelt. His brilliant personality and self-confidence in confronting the domestic crisis of the 1930's and the succeeding international crisis encouraged as great a delegation of power as any American Congress has ever granted. Legislative regret and resentment was already gathering force in the late 1930's. Pressure accumulated because of the insolence and brilliance of the exceptional group of energetic administrators and advisors whom the President gathered round him. The demand for a redress of the balance—for revenge against the disrespectful usurpers—grew through the 1930's and was scarcely held in check by the continuation of the crisis and the exceptional personality and political skill of President Roosevelt. Indeed, every time some stratagem of the President was successful, more fury was stored up. His replacement by Mr. Truman and the renaissance of demands for normality after the war released the flood of resentment which had been accumulating against the chief executive and the bureaucrats. Mr. Truman's bewilderment in the first phases of his administration encouraged it to surge forth. Thereafter, except in matters of foreign policy where President Truman was able to have his way by painting in its simplest and most dramatic terms the dangers of Soviet foreign policy, the legislative branch repeatedly showed its independence of the executive. It did so by blocking its proposed legislation, by overriding its vetoes and by conducting a furious campaign against it through abuse and investigations.

The first beginnings of the quest for loyalty in the executive branch began in the middle of President Roosevelt's second term, when the Congress which had been charmed and bemused by him was withdrawing its submission. The Dies Committee was the rallying point for this movement of Congress to disengage itself from the wiles of the executive. Beginning in 1938 with the charge that eight federal employees were said to be members of a Communist organization, the Dies Committee moved forward to more than 1,200 subversive government officials in 1941. Congressional distrust of the administration and their suspicion of its subversive inclinations were allayed during the war when the executive once more had the upper hand and when the bureaucracy swelled in numbers and grew in strength.

After the end of the war the relations between the legislative and the executive branches were increasingly colored by the antipathy of Congress towards the administration and its civil servants. The hatred of the administration was often displaced onto the civil servants who were more powerless and less capable of appealing to the electorate directly in the way the President was able to do. The civil servants could not protect themselves, and the legislative began a Roman holiday.

When the Republican administration acceded to power, the situation continued to be favorable to the legislative war on the civil service. The new President did not wish to interfere with Congress, and his party moreover had made its campaign in part by attacks on the socialistic and communistic character of the bureaucracy. It had promised that it would make war on Communism in the civil service, and Mr. McLeod's appointment to the State Department was only one of the invitations and concessions of the administration to the legislators' vengeful quest for subversion in the civil service.

It was only when the President saw his own prerogatives being encroached upon more and more seriously that he began to take some defensive action. The reassertion of a measure of Presidential leadership has slowed down the onslaught, but it has not ended the battle. It still goes on, despite the present lull. It cannot be otherwise as long as the legislative branch, by tradition, by organization and by social background is so distrustful of the bureaucracy and so long as there is a belief that bureaucrats keep secrets from legislators because they are bureaucrats and turn over secrets to enemy agents because they are engaged in a conspiracy.

III. Politicians and Intellectuals

The animus of the legislator against the bureaucrat is fed by another tension in American life: the tension between intellectuals and politicians. Although this country owes its creation as a state to intellectuals, there has been, ever since the Jacksonian revolution, a distrust of intellectuals in politics and a distrust of politics among intellectuals.

The practicing politician in the United States has not usually stood in deference to the intellectual. The small-town lawyer, full of old saws and vulgar jokes, shrewd and hard-headed, sharing and quick to flatter the prejudices of his constituents, is not a great respecter of the learned, the literary or the artistic. He is second to none in his appreciation of the state university and of the importance of a "good education," a "college education," in getting on with one's career and of amounting to something in life. The something to which the student should amount ought, however, to be more practical, more connected with everyday life, tougher and more manly than the reading and making of books. Pure scientific research and artistic creation are odd activities, difficult to understand in themselves and in their underlying motivations, and those who practice them do not seem to fit into the scheme of things in which the politician has confidence.

The local schoolteacher, the humblest representative of the intellectuals, is subjected to a stiff scrutiny by the town and village dignitaries. The parents who see in the teacher a rival authority are sometimes disturbed by an action or expression which their offspring attributes to the teacher. The teacher is often an outsider, at least in the sense of having been away to a normal school or a teachers' college, and might be reading a periodical otherwise unknown in the town. The teacher is suspected of being too distant, thinking he or she is better than the "ordinary people" of the place. Those more easily alarmed communicate their alarm to others.

What happens in the small town happens in far more complicated ways in the larger towns and big cities. At bottom, the image of the teacher remains prototypical—the teacher's job is not a man's job because it has to do with children, and the teacher is not perfectly in place in the community. University teachers, although the image is more complex, remain teachers and they are even more disquieting by the remoteness of their thoughts and sentiments.

The professional politician on the local level sometimes has a hard time with intellectuals. They, together with crusading journalists, are the reforming thorn in the side of the machine. They think they know better how to do things and they try to make life uncomfortable for him.

The atmosphere in which the politician has moved in his home town has usually been one in which lawyers, small and sometimes large businessmen, a few physicians and dentists, other politicians, real estate men set the tone. It is an atmosphere in which the concerns of intellectuals— scientific, literary, scholarly, and artistic—do not receive much attention, and if they do it is not apt to be very sympathetic. The businessmen with whom the politician associates in his home bailiwick read very little. Their wives are the readers and, if they can afford it, the patrons of literature and art such as it is. The play reading and book reviewing clubs of the provinces are the preserves of the ladies, and the men enter usually under duress. On the other side, the few intellectuals in the ordinary industrial city or market town hold themselves apart and aloof.

As the scene widens from local to state and then to national politics and administration, the intellectual becomes a more tangible reality to the politician. The complex tasks of administration on a larger scale make intellectuals, particularly university intellectuals trained in natural science, law and the social sciences, far more necessary as consultants and administrators than they were locally. This was true even before the New Deal and the changed relation between the federal civil service and the intellectuals. Intellectuals at this point become a very real problem. Far more than the politicians, they come more commonly from the great universities; they are more quick-witted, more knowledgeable, speak more rapidly and especially when young tend to give the impression of knowing very well what they are talking about. Many are Jewish, many are graduates of the Harvard Law School and many are both. It is not an easy matter for a politician who has spent his life in another environment to feel a warm sense of kinship with such people.

On top of all this, the politician now has to reckon with scientists; not the practical man at the State Agricultural and Mechanical college, but the most rarified of all intellectuals, mathematicians and physicists, theoretical and experimental, who must be entrusted with fantastically large sums of money and on whose quality or achievement no ordinary politician can pass judgment.

Even worse is the situation when these scientists must be allowed to possess the *secrets* on which the country depends. The politician, imbued to some extent with a populist outlook, is placed in a very difficult situation by the

present role of the scientist in national life. The very sentiments aroused by secrets—the fear and fascination of secrets
—are populistic sentiments, and populism is no lover of the
abstract scientist. Scientists with their willful ways, their
own world and their remoteness from the politician's world
stir anxiety in any case. Their great power arouses awe, but
their inheritance is resentment and the combination is a disturbing one to the politician and to the politician's relationship to the scientist. Furthermore, the impression which
more aggressive politicians could not fail to have that some
of the most eminent scientists were bothered by the use
on a massive scale of weapons built on the foundations of
their scientific knowledge has necessarily caused tension.
The politician's perception of the scientist's independent
judgment is not made more palatable by the scientist's great
self-esteem, especially at the top of the profession. The
most eminent scientists regard themselves as an elite while
politicians would be happier to view them as experts, i.e.,
as persons who happen to possess more specialized knowledge but who have no special moral ascendancy. The obvious
moral independence of the great scientist offends politicians
slightly, and in some cases, more than slightly.

The situation is not simplified by the political tradition
of the intellectual. For nearly one hundred years the intellectuals of this country identified themselves with the genteel tradition, a tradition which stood in conflict with the
rough-handed, florid-faced politics of the big city machines,
with the predominantly immigrant working classes of the
big cities on which they were based and the dour, com-
mercially minded farmers of the Middle West.

But those who lived in the light of the genteel tradition
had identified themselves with a cultural pattern which was
waning. A large section of the American intellectual classes
found themselves in opposition to most of the prospering
tendencies in American life. They felt a stronger kinship
with European cultural standards and practices and with
sections of the population of the Eastern seaboard—the Eastern "aristocracy"—which felt an inner sympathy with the

British pattern of life. Despite their criticisms of old Europe and their praise of the "new American Adam," American politics inspired the intellectuals with a feeling of repugnance.

The mode of discourse of American politics has always made for a little difficulty in the relations of the intellectuals and politicians. The uncouthness and crudity of the politician's conduct, the ham actor style of dress associated with his caricature, the extravagant and inflated style of speech, the pompous and polysyllabic vocabulary (at a time when, before the advent of social science, intellectuals still wrote in English) and their excessive aggressiveness of tone made intellectuals recoil somewhat from the politician and from politics.

Estranged from the robust and vulgar machine politics, they were often found in support of the municipal reformers who were so frequently locked in struggle with the local machines and their bosses.[1] They stood apart, too, from

1. How painful the American situation looked to our intellectuals when they thought of Great Britain. There the cream of the graduates of the two ancient universities entered the civil service by examinations which were delightfully archaic and which had no trace of spoils patronage about them. The role of unconscious and conscious considerations of status in the interview was often canvassed among the American intellectuals, and although it was criticized it did not impair the attractiveness of the system as a whole. To the many American intellectuals who imagined in horror aspirants calling, cap in hand, on a newly-elected politician or a party boss the day after an election to seek a place in the City Hall or in the State Capitol or in Washington, the British system seemed an intellectual's paradise. It offered what many American intellectuals desired: government service with a minimum of contact with or dependence on vulgar politicians. Even better, from the point of view of the American intellectual and Anglophile, and actually an important factor in the generally good relations of Parliament and the civil service, was the proximity in social status and education of the personnel of the two branches of government. Quite apart from the constitutional structure of the Parliamentary system, the British civil service in its administrative class were preponderantly graduates of Oxford and Cambridge and so, though rather less markedly, were the members of Parliament. Among liberal intellectuals, Professors Graham Wallas, R. H. Tawney, Harold J. Laski, G.D.H. Cole, Dr. Hugh Dalton, and the Webbs, provided an object delightful to contemplate. Politics, radical politics, conducted in a seemly fashion by the learned and reflective was wonderful. It was an ideal condition which was regretfully recognized as impossible to reproduce in the United States.

the energetic capitalistic enterprisers of the great periods of economic expansion which followed the Civil and First World Wars. In their repugnance for the practitioners of spoils politics, American academic intellectuals, inspired by Germany and Great Britain, had contributed greatly to the establishment of the merit system in the federal civil service as a means of curbing the depredations of the politicians.

Prior to the New Deal, the service of the federal government was not a profession which greatly attracted university graduates nor was the career of the American civil servant one which enjoyed the esteem of American intellectuals generally. The work was drab, its ends doubtful, its masters slightly alien.

Not all intellectuals by any means lived in the shade of the genteel tradition. There was already much intellectual hostility towards that tradition before the First World War, and afterwards the flood engulfed it. The flourishing populism of the quarter-century preceding 1914 had many intellectual adherents, but they differed from their Eastern and more genteel colleagues only in their flaming admiration for those repositories of virtue, i.e., the workers and farmers or only the latter. And despite the populists' contempt for their more genteel colleagues, in their contempt for machine politics, for corruption and the spoils system, they were one. The intellectual liberalism which drew its inspiration from Veblen, Dewey and Mencken and which opposed the genteel tradition was at least as antagonistic towards politics and politicians as the intellectuals whom they criticized. Although, with the exception of Mencken and a few of the literary men, these critics of American politics were not admirers of European institutions, their critical attitude towards America and the sympathy of some of them with the Russian Revolution of 1917 made it easy for some political antagonists, who regarded themselves as the vessels of American values, to label the critics as un-American.

The Great Depression saw the entry of the "intellectuals" into the federal government on an unprecedently large scale, and at an unprecedently rapid rate. The unpleasant shock to the legislator of the loss of his power to the bureaucracy was certainly not rendered easier to bear by the fact that it was being surrendered to intellectuals. The intellectuals in many instances regarded themselves as carrying on a form of "protected politics," politics in which the bruises of the political struggle could be borne by the Party leaders at the President's command while the actual shaping of political policy could safely be performed by the intellectuals in administrative posts. Administrative appointees were endowed with missionary zeal, and the political enemy was sometimes thought to be identical with the Congressman, who was either too reactionary or too stupid to understand what was called for. For the politician it was as if two enemies combined to become a single enemy; the hostility previously directed against separate enemies—bureaucrats and intellectuals—now coalesced on a single object.

IV. *The Alienated Intelligentsia*

The disruption of the order of governmental life and ultimately of public life during the past decade was facilitated when the two enemies, bureaucracy and the intellectuals which the New Deal and the war had brought together, appeared to unite with a third enemy, the enemy lurking at the edge of every populistic political fear, namely, the secret conspiratorial enemy. Why should the intelligentsia have become associated in the politician's mind with conspiracy? Like many of the phantasies of the populist politician, it is not entirely devoid of any correspondence with reality. It is certainly not an accurate representation of reality. It is a great distortion of real relationships, but it is a distortion and not a total fabrication.

For at least a quarter of a century, a sizeable fraction of the intellectuals who in Western countries were sympathetic with humanitarian reforms or with socialism tended to see in Soviet Communism a variant of democratic socialism which had temporarily gone off the main track of social progress in order to return further up the line at some future

date. The critics of Bolshevism, who spoke or wrote from a
very conservative or a stuffy trade union point of view,
seemed so much out of sympathy with the Bolshevik pretensions to stand for social justice that they had little moral
credit. The official socialist parties in Europe held themselves aloof from the Soviet Union during the twenties and
thirties and struggled hard to keep themselves from being
bested by the Communist parties in their respective countries. There were, of course, small bands of dissidents within
the socialist parties who were more pro-Soviet and who demanded close co-operation with the Communist parties,
but the leadership was usually successful in keeping them
under control. The obvious partisanship of many of the
Social Democratic detractors and the lack of humanitarian
sympathies of the anti-Socialists made the realistic assessment of Bolshevism very difficult.

The Great Depression of the 1930's, the Spanish Civil
War, and the establishment of National Socialism, occurred
against a background which made the realistic understanding of Bolshevism especially difficult. The 1920's had almost
extinguished political activity and intense political interests
among American intellectuals. It was the decade of the
Babbitt and of the Teapot Dome scandal, of the degradation
of Bryan in the Scopes trial, of the Sacco-Vanzetti case and
the Prohibition fiasco—nearly everything tended to make
American intellectuals feel that politics was rotten and hope-
less, politicians knaves and fools.

The major events of the 1930's could quite reasonably be
interpreted as evidence that the traditional ruling groups
of party politicians, industrialists, bankers and the legal profession were failing to deal adequately with economic problems, and many intellectuals, already disposed by long tradition and recent experience to take a critical attitude
towards their own authorities, fell an easy prey to the propaganda of the Communists regarding the efficiency and
justice of the rulers of the Soviet society, "the land without
unemployment."

Especially among intellectuals, who had taken little inter-

est or part in politics before the depression, the contempt
and aversion which on the whole they felt towards their own
politicians and their horror at the facts of widespread unemployment and the consolidation of National Socialism,
there was a tendency, once they became interested in politics, to be impatient with the roundaboutness of representative democracy. Not having been greatly attracted by the
resourcefulness of representative institutions and unreflect-
ively taking their personal and civil liberties for granted,
many intellectuals whose latent humanitarianism had been
aroused by unemployment and Nazi anti-Semitism, did not
see any grounds for complaint against the methods of the Soviet political leaders. These seemed to them to be more benevolent and perhaps fundamentally more truly democratic
than those in their own countries. Newly aroused to an urgent sense of the injustice of their own society, and more concerned with results than with methods, the obvious devia-
tion of the Bolshevik elite from the "purely formal liberties"
of bourgeois democracy did not strike many young and a
smaller number of older American intellectuals as very important, even where they were willing to recognize that they
were real. The inexperience of youth or the naiveté of adult-
hood against a background of distrust of political authority
made it easy for them to accept the Communist conception
of politics as a conspiracy behind a façade—the immoral conspiracy of Wall Street or the City of London against the
moral and desirable conspiracy of the Communist Party.
Their naiveté about human motives, a product of youth in
many instances and of a deeper moral blindness in others,
and especially their ignorance of the motives and spirit of
political life as it is lived by politicians and civil-minded
citizens and their belief in the wickedness and power of
businessmen, made them willing victims of the economism
of the Communists. Once they came to think that "economic
motives" are all-determining, the plausibility of the Communist outlook was further confirmed.

Having previously been uninterested in liberty but en-
joying it, without using their political rights, they readily

came to believe that whereas in Western countries citizens possessed only empty political rights which they could not use for any substantial end, in the Soviet Union they had "economic freedom." Becoming sensitive to the wickedness of racial discrimination, they saw the existence of racial discrimination in America and in the European colonial empires, and eagerly believed that the Soviet Union gave full equality to all its ethnic groups. It was a simple step to move on to a condemnation of all imperialistic expansion at the expense of backward peoples—again, a good article of American faith—and to share the Communist denunciation of imperialism. Again, ignorance and an enthusiastic will to believe caused the Soviet Union to be accepted as the one great power which was not imperialistic.

Another of the identities of American populism and Bolshevism which caused a politically naive intelligentsia to feel sympathy for the Communist line was the alleged openness of Soviet diplomacy. Ever since Lenin's direct appeals to the workers in foreign capitalist countries over the heads of their rulers and Litvinov's proposals for drastic disarmaments in the League of Nations, Bolshevik procedures in international relations had enjoyed a high esteem from those Western intellectuals who were repelled by the "undemocratic" secrecy and the ritualistically rule-bound methods of traditional diplomacy. Traditional diplomacy with its confidentiality, its detailed negotiations over small issues, its reputation for old-world deviousness, its monopoly by the upper classes, its lack of personal force and color, has never appealed to the populist element in American society—the intellectuals no more than anyone else. The American intellectuals, when they had broken loose from the genteel tradition and from the cultural hegemony of the Eastern seaboard and when they decided, too, to renounce the anti-political aesthetic outlook of the 1920's, found Bolshevism very appealing in this respect. It was like the rediscovery of their own attitudes in a fresh and vigorous form, appropriate to the frightening crisis of the time.

Then, too, the content of Soviet foreign policy was

morally gratifying. Soviet intervention in the Spanish Civil War when the United States declared an embargo on the export of armaments and France and Great Britain adhered to a policy of nonintervention, was widely accepted as evidence of the wholesome purposes of Soviet foreign policy and of the freedom of the Soviet elite from hypocrisy and narrow self-interest. The Communist denunciation of fascism, which far exceeded in vigor that which came from official circles of the Western democracies, strengthened the tendency to idealize the Soviet elite. It was, after all, the shock of the National Socialist triumph in Germany which had helped to "politicize" the American intellectuals, and the Soviet Union, among the powers, and the Communist Party among the parties, were the most vehement denouncers of Nazism and Fascism.

Intellectuals with their feelings of being "outside" politics at a time when they wanted to be in the movement for humanitarian reforms were compliant victims of the special praise for scientists and intellectuals which Communist propaganda stressed. The obviously important role played by authors and theorists in the public phases of Communist Party life made it extremely appealing.

Neither the Republican nor the Democratic Party had a periodical like *The New Masses* where cultural affairs were discussed in extremely serious tones and where books were treated as if they made a difference. *Collier's* and *The Saturday Evening Post* did not treat cultural matters so, even though they were no longer the Babbitt magazines they had been in the 1920's. The Communists claimed to be guided by "principles" and "theory," and intellectuals like to see events in terms of principles and theories. That is what underlies their scientific achievements, but it has contributed to the widening of the gulf between them and empirical American politics which by the avoidance of theories and principles diminishes the frictions which are inevitable in a heterogeneous large-scale society. Leninism stressed the importance of "correct theory" for "correct practice," and the Communists have never allowed "theoretical" issues to lie dormant. The Party produced a vast literature expounding the theory and applying it to concrete situations. Those who felt the need—as many young people did at that time—to see the world in an ordered way, in which every event is interpreted within the framework of a more comprehensive view, found the Communist Party an organization worthy of sympathy and even membership.

The Party had bookshops, it had theaters, it even had a few films. It had clubs for intellectuals and parties galore. It offered the opportunity and the trap of a totally comprehensive round of life, allegedly dominated by the ideal. The claims of Communists to represent social justice and the constant stress that the Soviet Union as a whole and Communists in each country were the victims of subtle or cruel bourgeois persecution preyed upon tender consciences and prevented realistic criticism. The fear of being a "Red baiter" caused many a critical thought to be suppressed. The background of many middle-class intellectuals in the United States and in other countries, too, made them into almost "natural" Stalinists, even where they did not join the Party —as relatively few of them did.

Seeing their own societies as demoralized and disintegrating, they nurtured ideals of societies highly integrated in purposes and beliefs. When they looked at Soviet society they thought they saw a society dominated by an almost unanimously shared purpose. Unemployment among university graduates and the fear of war aroused by Nazi and Fascist bellicosity made them the dupes of the Communist argument that science was being used to destroy man or that it was itself being suppressed by political interference. Firm believers in the rightness of applying science to man's problems—good American beliefs—they believed that in the Soviet Union science was being lovingly fostered for the service of man. The belief, very much at home in American populism, that popular revolutions are always just, permitted the Communists to create and exploit feelings of guilt concerning the Allied intervention during the Russian Civil War.

The belief in the injustices of their own rulers fostered a concurrent belief that the rulers of the Soviet Union were making a worthy and generous effort to raise the condition of mankind to higher levels of well-being and dignity. A group of hard-headed men, their minds focused on a high and remote ideal, demanding much from others and unsparing on themselves while driving ahead with all of the resources of natural and social science to transfigure and elevate the life of man on earth—this was the Communist picture of the Soviet elite. In the course of the 1930's, this image came to possess the thought, not only of Party members but of many persons of considerable education and apparently independent judgment who in a time of great crisis saw in idealistic selflessness, purposefulness and efficiency based on "science," the highest virtues of public life. Communism appealed to people who were impatient with convention and tradition and who responded to the crisis with doctrinaire rationalism of certain types of intellectuals. For those who were repelled by the stereotyped rhetoric, the compromise, and the *bonhomie* of politicians in the City Hall, the State House and the Capitol, who found their own politicians fumbling and who needed the appearance of decisive action, the Bolshevik elite appeared to be the incorporation of the ideal. Bolshevism was a form of "highbrow" technocracy, it was the management of a large society without politicians and without the dirty work of politics. Here too the American intelligentsia was the victim of a more pervasive American populistic attitude, namely, the belief in the superfluity and wickedness of the politician. But instead of demanding the direct rule of the people expressed through great leaders, in the style of the older American populism, the anti-political populism of the intellectuals accepted uncritically Communist populism—the formula of the dictatorship of the proletariat. The affinities were sufficiently close not to strain a willing intelligence.

The anomalies of the Moscow trials and the great purges alienated some Party members and fellow-travellers, who were always unstable in any case. The vast majority of those who had fallen for the Communist line out of their own "natural" populistic predisposition to Stalinism aggravated by the frivolousness of youthful or adult naiveté remained true, however, to their new faith. They found indeed many ingenious or remarkably simple-minded arguments to justify it. Only the Soviet-German Pact and the Soviet attack on Finland shook the fellow-travellers and the broader mass of Stalinoid non-Communists. After June, 1941, the Stalinoid mentality more than recouped its losses. A mixture of anxiety and then of relief at the gradually stiffening Soviet resistance and bad conscience for having judged so harshly an ally who had been so cruelly attacked, was exploited by a fierce Communist propaganda offensive to rehabilitate the image of the benevolent, realistic, forceful and efficient rulers of the Soviet Union.

Despite the disillusioning effect of Soviet conduct immediately after the war, the Communists still retained their influence over many of their intellectual followers. The peculiar incapacity of extremists to attend to anything except extremists and their incapacity to perceive or understand moderate points of view helped to keep some of the intelligentsia enthralled by Communism. The fury and irrationality of the extremist anti-Communists helped the cause of Communism because their conduct seemed to confirm the erroneous interpretation of bourgeois politics which the Communists foisted onto their dupes. The hatred of humanitarian reform expressed by the extremists confirmed the simplistic view of the fellow-travellers and party members among the intellectuals that the "bourgeoisie" or "Wall Street" whose voice they heard in the extremist ranting was completely reactionary. The carryings-on of the Hearst papers and of certain legislative committees interpreted in the doctrinaire perspective of the left-wing intelligentsia seemed to prove that the Leninist-Stalinist diagnoses were correct. The wild methods and extreme overstatements of most vigorous anti-Communists made it difficult for the victims of the Communist hoax to clear their heads. The mere fact that anti-Communism used, as in the case of the House Committee on Un-American Activities, such disreputable methods and was so indiscriminate and violent in its accusations, hid the grain of truth in its vituperation and rendered suspect its acceptance.

Gradually, under the impact of Soviet expansion after the war, and the completion of the evidence, long more than ample, of the thoroughgoing subservience of Communist Parties in all countries to Soviet foreign policy, the attachment of the intellectuals who had once found a haven there came practically to an end.

In retrospect it is clear that in many of its basic attitudes the leftist intelligentsia of the 1930's was very American indeed. It shared and adapted that strand of the American tradition which is so powerful that it influences reactionaries like McCarthy and left-wing radicals and great upper-class personalities like Franklin Roosevelt. The reason why many American intellectuals were able to support the New Deal and to sympathize with the Communist Party in the 1930's was not because the New Deal was dominated by Communists. It was rather that both movements corresponded to a fundamental tendency in American political thought and sentiment which is very far from being confined to the intellectuals, namely, distrust of professional and party politicians, impatience with the traditional legal and political institutions which intervene between the people's desires and their execution by their elected representatives, belief in the moral superiority of the people, and a suspicion of privacy and withdrawal from the common culture.

Still alienated, the once radical intellectuals have by now renounced the Communist Party or its affiliates as sources of moral and intellectual guidance. Only a few party hacks remain and only a handful of these came into the movement after 1935. The great movement of deception initiated in 1934 and sanctioned by the Seventh Congress of the Communist International in the following year has faded away among the intelligentsia.

But the intellectuals are still not at ease in this society.

The fundamental factors which underlay their pre-Communist alienation from politics and politicians are still at work. Despite efforts to make themselves at home in American political life, many American intellectuals still find themselves "outsiders" in their relation to politics. They are less outsiders than they used to be, but still the feeling of being an outsider remains in many hearts.

The past twenty-five years have seen a real change in the role of the intellectual in this country. He has acquired powers and positions which were earlier impossible. With reluctance the rulers of American society—political, economic and military—have been forced to acknowledge the relevance of the intellectual, and from his own side the intellectual has sought to incorporate himself into American society, in sentiment as well as function.

The 1930's with all their vices and silliness were the period also of an increased sense of political responsibility. The Stalinism of the American intelligentsia was in a sense a fever which preceded and announced the prospect of recovery from the apolitical and anti-political attitudes of nearly a century. Postwar anti-Communist extremism and especially Senator McCarthy and the excesses of the obsession with security and hyperloyalty have undone some of the incipient cure, but not entirely. Intellectuals in the United States now do accept the idea of government service as a normal and honorable career and not just as a refuge for drones. They still do not lend themselves readily to the idea of a political career, although there are now, as there has almost always been, some very striking exceptions to this rule. For the first time since the war of 1914-1918, American intellectuals are being moved by a desire to be incorporated into their national culture.[2]

The Communist and fellow-traveller movement has never been a serious threat to American society. Except for the

---

2. The distance still to be traversed may be seen in the symposium arranged by the *Partisan Review* several years ago on *Our Country and Our Culture.* Good will and eagerness did not overcome the long tradition of withdrawal and alienation.

aid it has provided for Soviet espionage, it has probably never been harmful to the institutional system of this country. To this there is one exception.[3] The Communist movement and its inroads among the intellectuals in the 1930's have done harm because they reinforced the breach between the politicians and the intellectuals. What was the Communist movement if not an aggressive and noisy vote of non-confidence in the capacity and probity of the leaders of our political system? Such an offense worked injury to the sentiments of self-esteem of the politician in the United States. Politicians are hypersensitive men, not always accurately or justly sensitive, but certainly hypersensitive, especially to implications of disapproval. They could hardly be other than sensitive to the disapproval of the intellectuals, disapproval on grounds of vulgarity, corruption, incompetence, evil intentions, inhumanity and moral worthlessness.

In their most extreme forms we have seen the response to these implied insults in the Congressional investigations into security and loyalty and in the pressure of the legislative branch on the executive in security and loyalty policy.

V. *The Embitterment of Opposition*

The balance of the political parties themselves had also had an inflaming effect.

Most of the difficulties which have arisen in recent years carry to excess qualities which in themselves are good and desirable. Fundamentalism is the product of an excessive attachment to traditional institutions and beliefs, the validity of which is endangered. In a less extreme form the attachment is a source of stability. Xenophobia is a vice grown out of a virtue; it is the shadowy margin of our achievement in the assimilation of so many diverse peoples into a single nation. Our isolationism, that is, our anti-Europeanism, is

---

3. Another casualty of the Communist movement is youthful radicalism. The spontaneous generosity and idealism of youthful rebellion have been exploited and defaced by their involvement with the ugly heritage of Communist scheming.

the fruit of an excessively energetic turning of the back on archaic conventions and on the etiquette of inequality. Populism has grown out of the excesses of equality, of a critical attitude towards authority, of the self-esteem of the ordinary people, all of which in proper measure are virtues quintessential to the well-being of a democracy. The mania for publicity is an excrescence of the politician's respect for the opinion of the electorate; while the prying desire to expose is a malignant outgrowth of the freedom of the press and the journalistic profession's insistence on its exercise. The alienation of the intelligentsia is a costly and excessive development of the necessary autonomy of the various professions and of the devotion to the cultivation of their own values.

In a somewhat similar fashion, the party system and the separation of powers, central constituents of a free society, have contributed to the present disturbance. The Republican Party, after twelve years in office, was removed from its control of the federal government under humiliating conditions in the election of 1932. Then it was kept from power for a succession of three terms in which the Democratic Party introduced many reforms which injured the deepest moral sense of the more traditionalistic sections of the Republican Party and fought a war which many Republican believed had been brought on by irresponsible and even conspiratorial internationalist machination. In the fourth and especially in the fifth terms of the Democratic presidency the country approached a political stalemate. The presidency was Democratic, but in each House of Congress the numerical balance of Republicans and Democrats was so close and there were so many dissident Democrats that the Republicans had the veto power. Then in the 80th Congress the Republicans had the majority in both houses. By their bargaining and obstructive power and the energy with which they fought, they were by no means an opposition confined to criticism of the Democratic administration. A substantial minority in the Democratic Party in Congress consisted of Southern Democrats, who, although by no means all fearful of subversion, and free of the tradition of isolationism, had their hatchets out for the Northern intellectuals, trade unionists and their urban machine allies whom they disliked for agitating the question of Negro rights. Southern populism has many of the same qualities as Middle Western populism — fundamentalism, hyperequalitarianism — and it was easy for it to collaborate with the Republican Party. Furthermore, the Republicans were encouraged by the belief that the malaise with which the country was experiencing the world favored their prospects. They were beginning to feel more in tune with broader political sentiment than they had for a long time. The growing apprehension about the atomic bomb, the dangers of espionage, the costliness of rearmament and of economic and military aid to Europe, then the grief, humiliation and anxiety of the apparently unending Korean War, all made the Republicans feel that the political tide was turning in their direction. Power began to loom closer; it began to appear attainable once more. Passion for office stirred the Republican soul, the blood ran more vigorously in their veins as the thought of returning to power became more immediate and more plausible to them. They became ravenous. So long out of power and so close to it! Anything short of insurrection might have appealed to many Republicans as a way of getting back.

This happens even in the most dignified of parliamentary families. In Great Britain the Labour majority in the last Labour Government was so slight that their position resembled the position of the Democratic administration in the United States. The Conservatives tried in the spring of 1951 to drive the Labour Government from power by a series of "prayers" which required the Labour Party to have its maximum voting strength present at all times, day and night, because a lost division might bring down the government. For a time the Labour Party was even having to bring some of its members out of hospitals in order to be able to retain its majority.

For the Republicans, investigation and denunciation of

the Roosevelt-Truman regime seemed an ideal instrument with which to batter a fortress already breached by a rising restiveness. The revelations of Miss Bentley and Mr. Chambers, the conviction of Alger Hiss, the detection of Miss Judith Coplon in the act of handing classified documents to a Soviet official, the Gold-Greenglass-Sobel-Rosenberg trials gave an air of verisimilitude to the charge that the Democrats had been treasonable, and if not treasonable at least complacent in the face of treason.

It seemed to be a marvelous political instrument. It was so good, and the bumbling House Committee on Un-American Activities, especially after Martin Dies was defeated and its newest chairman, Parnell Thomas, was jailed for corrupt practices, seemed so incapable of taking advantage of the possibility, that there was a general movement of interest, when Senator McCarthy in 1950 announced that he had in his possession at the time a long list of members of the Communist Party inside the Department of State. It was not long before Senator McCarthy's irrepressible vigor, his quick-witted evasiveness, his skill in throwing dust into the eyes of his opponents became apparent. He had been only a bumptious nobody at first, and without the aid and encouragement of his seniors of the Republican Party in the Senate he could not have become much more than that. He was given patronage, opportunities, and encouragement. The encouragement which he received from the elders of his own party was not always a result of their complete agreement with him. It rested rather on the belief that he might do some damage to the Democrats if allowed to persist in his attacks.[4]

---

4. The acceptance of Senator McCarthy by those politicians who normally would have little traffic with such a man, who felt uneasy during the alliance and who finally, very anxiously, dropped him, was rendered easier by the similarities of his mode of speech and the characteristic mode of American political discourse. American political language is notoriously rough and uncivil. Senator Dirksen was right when he said that the McCarthy party had only spoken in the "grand old American way." The natural disposition of the small-town politicians, far away from the centers of gentility and eager to distinguish themselves from it, was to speak very col-

As his talent was revealed and his powers grew, the respectable conservatives within the party began to discover that the man they were promoting might end by overshadowing them all. As long as he confined himself to the Democrats, to intellectuals and to Communists he could do only good. It was also becoming clear that he was a resourceful fighter and that there seemed to be loud public support for him. It appeared dangerous to criticize or oppose him. His successive triumphs and his persistence on the front page made those who did not share his views afraid to dissent from him for fear that their constituents would think that they were falling too far out of step with Senator McCarthy, and that they were not sufficiently anti-Communist. He set the standards for the young politicians who sought to make their way in Congress. Even outstanding Democrats were reluctantly unwilling to vote against the appropriations for his committee when he was at the height of his power, even though they made many speeches against him, in and out of Congress.

In the end Senator McCarthy was brought down by the respectable bulwarks of conservatism in the Senate, both Democratic and Republican, and the decision of the Presi-

loquially and strongly. The belief that the audience must be impressed, the tradition of the damnation and hellfire preaching of the revivalist fundamentalism, and a conviction that only if one did not appear to be a dude could one win the votes of the common people have all contributed to make American political speech exceptionally rude and aggressive.

Political campaigns in all countries and the attendant need to stir the ordinary people tends to introduce an unwonted measure of forcefulness into political speeches. In populistic America the preferences and expectations of the common people were more catered to by orators than they were in other countries. In addition to this, American politicians came from the people and talked to the people more than the politicians of other countries. They spoke the language of the people, coarsened by the roughness of the politicial campaign.

Accordingly, American parliamentary and campaign language became and has remained rather aggressive and melodramatic in tone. Senator McCarthy, although his basic outlook was really quite different from the outlook of the ordinary Congressman or Senator sounded more like them than he really was. He appeared to be only a more forceful speaker, a more colorful and more outspoken critic of the inner enemy, the tamperers with the secrets of defense and the secret withholders of loyalty, than his fellow legislators.

dent that his arrogance was intolerable and hurtful. During
most of the four years of his tyrannical ascendancy in American political life he owed his success to his own qualities and
to the readiness of the press, radio and television to satisfy
his need for oceans of publicity.

The initial success of his upward struggle he owes, however, to the desperate eagerness of the stalwarts of the Republican Party in Congress and in the Republican National
Committee to seize on any stick with which to beat the
administration dog. The greatly extended popularity of the
pursuit of Communists and spies by violent denunciation
during Senator McCarthy's ascendancy is to some extent
the result of his obvious personal success. It is also the
result of the Republican belief that it was the only way to
get the Democrats out of power and to keep them out.

It used to be said that European socialist parties, by
being permanently in opposition, had become doctrinaire
and unrealistic. This is just as true of parties with a long
history of being in power, when they have been too long in
opposition. Prolonged opposition drives a party towards irresponsibility. Proximity to power after long opposition over-
heats the passions and brings irrational prejudices and animosities to the surface. The long exile of the Republican
Party from office weakened the inhibitions which respectability and civility impose on populism. In that situation
Senator McCarthy became the chosen instrument of a proto-
McCarthyite state of mind.

VI. *The Burden of the Politician:*
The Vociferous Minority

The politician's background is also his audience. The
audience is not homogeneous and not all parts are equally
resonant to the politician's voice and action. Some are more
active in forming the politician's image of his constituency
than others, and it is to this image that he addresses himself.

Just how much of his constituency does the politician
know at first hand? Certainly very little. The territorial ex-

tent of a Congressional constituency is large in most states while for the Senators the constituency is a whole state, which in the most populistic regions is very large indeed. The average population of the Congressional constituency is very much larger than any with which a man can be in first-hand contact. It has, on the average, more than four times the population of a British parliamentary district.

When he does return to "mend his fences" he cannot see very many ordinary citizens. He sees the party bosses, the functionaries and the "militants" and he sees occasional persons at dinners or in bars, in grocery stores or hotel lobbies. Much of the time he himself is doing the speaking and when he meets random individuals it is for no more than an introduction or a handshake. Except for friends and fellow party leaders he is likely to see only those who are sufficiently insistent to push their way through to him. These may be persons who are seeking his aid on some personal problem or who wish to invite his support for some communal project or a local interest.

The political interest in the larger society which they encounter tends to be the interest of zealots with bees in their bonnets, persons who are intensely and often angrily concerned with international or national problems. Likewise when he is in Washington his communications from his public will on the whole be solicitations for aid in connection with some problem the individual encounters in his relations with the goverment, or they express very strong political opinions, often of an extreme sort. The legislator seldom receives disinterested mail about general legislative problems.

The persons with strong views come from all social and educational classes. Abusive letters, passionately worded letters, come in pencil, crabbedly or madly written on sheets of ruled paper torn from school children's copybooks, or they might come written with a flourish or neatly typed on elegant personal stationery. There seem to be more of the former than of the latter, but there are enough of all kinds to justify the view that angry passions and embittered abuse are not confined to a single class. Prim little clerks, rough laborers, suspicious schoolteachers, prosperous and resentful janitors, well-dressed housewives in their early fifties, splenetic cigar-chewing businessmen and the nervous secretaries of building and loan associations can all be obsessed with the wickedness of bureaucrats and intellectuals and foreigners and Communists. It is these and people like them who make up the nativist lunatic fringe so much in the field of vision of certain Congressmen.

Obsessed with powerful prejudices, xenophobic, stridently patriotic, aggressively suspicious of the stealers of secrets and the subversive agents of the "Rosenfeld revolution," seeing Jews, bankers and Bolsheviks in a single ring operating behind every political event, this rag, tag and bobtail of American political life make a noise very disproportionate to their voting power. The passionate letter writers and telegraphers are seldom organized; when they are, they are loosely and inefficiently organized. They are a small, cranky, and rambling body of spinsters, "lumpen" proletarians, fly-by-night promoters, unsuccessful businessmen, toughs with political notions, solitaries and strays, beset by personal misery and thinking only of salvation through politics. These are the pickets who used to be seen marching up and down in front of the White House.

Actually, very few Congressmen share their views. Some, however, who are out of close contact with their immense constituencies and who are lacking in self-confidence, make the mistake of believing that these pathetic people represent the normal majority of the electorate. And for those who have found it necessary to shout into the far-reaching void, the resonance provided by the lunatic fringes has been both welcome and misleading.

The politician who has listened to this vocal minority comes to believe, or if he already shares some of their beliefs, has reinforced, their conspiratorial conception of politics. He believes not only that there has been a real communist conspiracy abroad in the world, but that it has penetrated throughout the whole of American political, social, and economic life. Even if he does not believe completely in the conspiratorial view, he hastens to "put it on" for he thinks that that is what is required for political success. It thus becomes the conventional language of political life, even for those to whom it does not come naturally. It has become a quasi-official illusion, a collective representation which many who have not shared it have felt that they must nonetheless acknowledge.

VII. *The Temptation of the Politician:*
Populism and Publicity

The ethos of American politics, its orientation towards the constituent and the concern of the politician to keep himself before the public's eye is exaggerated by the institutions of mass communication. The popular press provides a temptation and an opportunity for populistic politicians because it gives them a way of reaching much larger numbers of persons than they could reach by direct speech, even in the largest mass meetings.

Whereas in the nineteenth century, apart from the church the politician had little competition from other public institutions for the attention of the mass of the population insofar as it concerned itself with events transpiring outside its immediate sphere, the twentieth-century politician has had to compete with the other attractions offered first by the popular press, then by the films, and more recently by radio and television entertainment. In the nineteenth century, before vaudeville, politics was the major public spectacle for the mass of the urban population; it was their entertainment and their excitement. Cock-fighting was only for a few, bear-baiting had died out, boxing had not yet become popular and football and baseball had not yet become the great organized activities engaging the attention of millions of people. Religious revivals occasionally stirred great numbers, but only politics offered recurrent and steady diversion. Not the issues but the personalities, and above all the aggressiveness and thrill of the contest aroused the populace. Now these functions are also performed by other institutions.

The popular press, which gave the politician the chance to reach so many people, also gave him a new set of competitors to outdo, or at least to match in attractiveness. With the development of the popular press and the popular entertainment industries, the mass of the population came to be served by a profession whose skills were directed towards excitement and entertainment rather than edification or instruction. This meant that politics was viewed from the standpoint of this profession. The populistic politician already devoted to histrionic oratory and to the melodramatic representation of issues and alternatives adapted himself quite easily to the expectations of those who mediated his relations with his larger public.

It is not that the politician tried to be an athletic hero or a film star or a criminal. Rather it was the new technique of reporting, the tone of the news in the popular press which was interested in sensation, in the dramatic and the scandalous, that influenced the tone of political discourse. The journalist, experienced in a variety of fields of reporting before becoming a political journalist, brought into political reporting an imagery and a conception of the world which pushed politics into the direction of melodrama and crisis. The strenuous rat-race of American journalism brings to the fore men whose first interest has often been sport, or crime or local politics and whose professional skill has been developed through dramatic descriptions of prize fights, baseball games, and crimes and their detection. The popular journalist's belief that the popular audience could become interested in an event only if it were at the most intense level of melodrama marches hand in hand with the journalist's own professional view that the world is a melodrama and that practically all that falls outside the extremes is dead, stale stuff which can interest no one and which is of no significance. Many journalists match this interest in sensations with a febrile enthusiasm for their work, for bigger and better shows, scoops, and "inside stories." They act on the basis of the belief that the world was created to provide a series of newsworthy and reportable events. Everything is fair game for them. The professional pride in scoops and in unique, individual "angles" tends, with a few exceptions, to work against sober reporting and to accentuate the melodramatic elements in public life. The journalist is on the lookout for dirty linen—and for someone who wishes it washed in public. The tradition of the muckraking reporter adds a specifically political note to the more comprehensive sensationalism of the popular press, which constitutes most of the press. The journalist makes his name by finding out the private or secret things which someone else has no desire to disclose.

Thus the politician's need for gaining the attention of his constituency and the broader public, to show that he is alive to their needs and is serving their interests, as well as because he measures his own success in terms of the publicity he can achieve, is met half-way by the journalist's professional and often personal interest in disclosing everything which is not normally disclosed to the public.

The American press is proud of its record in muckraking and in the protection of the public interest. It is jealous of the freedom which allows it to make so many disclosures. Restraint—even self-restraint—is viewed, with a professional bias, as a desertion of the public interest. Journalists as well as politicians justify their mania for publicity in terms of a populistic democratic theory that the people must know everything and judge accordingly.

Politicians and administrators are constantly before the public in press conferences, on the telephone, on television and radio programs and in newsreels to give their views on all of the great issues of war and peace. Radio and television interviews, articles in the popular weeklies, are much sought after by politicians as sources of income and more importantly as means of publicity. Politicians sound off on every subject on which they can get an audience or which they think will attract an audience. They are forced to speak on matters on which they may have few ideas or knowledge, and in which the effect is obtained by the forcefulness and extremity of the views expressed and the conceptions presented. A considerable proportion of American politicians openly exploit or comply with this situation. They deem it both right and necessary. They need it to reach their constituents and they enjoy it too. It fits into their ideology.

Debate in Congress is accordingly weakened in favor of press conferences in the legislator's office. Diplomatic consultations and negotiations are hampered by the legislator's belief in the rightfulness and necessity of unlimited publicity.

The people—not all, of course, but many of those who are interested in politics—are suspicious and curious about what goes on "on the inside." The public's distrust of politicians, their expectation that politicians if left alone will be "up to some dirty work," and their fascination by power and its exercise offers reward to the journalist who can tell them about what goes on where their unaided eyes cannot easily see.

Politicians compete, therefore, for the aid and friendliness of journalists. They wish to stand in well with the journalists, with those who can affect so vitally all they are interested in and to which they are sensitive. To those whose sustenance is publicity, good relations with those who can give them that publicity are matters of life and death. The politicians themselves like to "leak," to show that they are in the possession of important information which journalists would like to know. It shows that they are "on the inside," that they possess valuable secrets, and it shows the journalists that they are worth listening to and helping.[5]

---

5. The friendliness of politicians towards the merchants of publicity is not unqualified. It is perhaps not accidental that of Senator McCarthy's great campaigns two of them were against publicity and propaganda agencies. It may well be that they were chosen because they were easy marks and unable to defend themselves. Perhaps they were easy marks because so much is expected from publicity and propaganda by politicians and so little can ever be demonstrated as effective results. The propagandists who broadcast to foreign countries or who conduct libraries and information programs cannot harm the politician, so he has no need to be as propitiatory

This incontinent publicity is justified by those who are parties to it, by the invocation of the public interest. The politicians, much as they are drawn to the extreme pole of publicity, also know that not all this publicity is conducive to the public good. They know that not everything ought to be disclosed.

The pressure of publicity sets going a counterpressure for the safeguarding of secrecy. As sometimes occurs in the ambivalent orientation towards contradictory extremes, the responsibility for the maintenance of complete secrecy is put on someone else by those who themselves practice publicity with passionate devotion and a split conscience. The more they talk, therefore, the more they insist that others be silent. The more they talk about secrets, about the fascinating, mysterious secrets on which so much depends and the more curious they themselves are about these secrets, the more they insist that others must keep them, not from themselves but from still others.

Both constitutionally and personally, politicians are against secrecy. They cannot stand secrets being withheld from themselves and they insist that others be deprived of their possession by complete publicity and by rigorous security. They cannot claim that the journalists should keep them, given their identity of viewpoint with the journalists. The brunt of the pressure for secrecy and publicity is solved by going in both directions at once: maximum disclosure by politicians, maximum secrecy by administrators, but not towards politicians. This fascination with the extremes becomes a disturbing paradox when it is the very same information that is to be kept both secret and made public at the same time. This paradox is regularly on view in the legislators who agitate furiously for the stiffest security measures and who insist on hyperloyalty, but who are always "leaking" confidential information to the press.

It takes an intense form in the Congressional investigat-

---

as he is towards domestic publicists. Hence Senator McCarthy and his friends could abuse the staff of agencies whose responsibility for publicity entranced them.

ing committee and in the Congressional agitation about security. It reached its peak in the repeated temptation to investigate the Central Intelligence Agency and in the interest in investigating scientists. Those who hold secrets must be given the maximum of publicity. The unattainability of their secrets makes them all the more fascinating.

Many forces come to a head here: the preoccupation with secrecy and the love of being on the inside, the love of secrets and the fear of secrets; xenophobia, anti-intellectualism, the suspicion of sophisticated ways and the fear of clandestine activities; isolationism and the desire to make a good impression on one's constituents; being on good terms with journalists and taking revenge on bureaucrats. Above all it is the focus of the hyperpatriotic sentiments, which accentuate the passion and sensitivity with which the two incompatibles of secrecy and publicity are pursued.

VIII. Concluding Remarks

The alarm about espionage and subversion is not all of one piece. Just as a phenomenon like populism or isolationism has more than one motive, so the various factors which we have enumerated in the course of this chapter come together into different combinations. Some persons might see the Communists more as foreigners, some might be more worried about the unreliability of intellectuals and others more worried about atomic and hydrogen bombs. In some, anti-Semitism may play some part in the attraction of anti-Communism, in others a distrust of the Eastern seaboard. Fundamentalist Protestantism, narrow Roman Catholicism or a Judaism trying to prove itself more royalist than the king, might all end up with the same point of view.

Likewise, the strength of the various factors varies in intensity. In some persons the alarm is genuine but mild and appears in consciousness only occasionally; in other persons it is literally an obsession.

All the factors, however, which we have mentioned, work

generally in the same direction, even though some incline more to one object, e.g., the universities or scientists, another more to civil servants. All are permeated by the same fundamental disposition and all drive, in varying ways, against the principles of the pluralistic, civil society.

PART III

Consequences

CHAPTER 6

THE DEFORMATION OF CIVILITY

I. The Pluralistic Society: The Separation and Co-operation of the Spheres

THE PREOCCUPATION with subversion and secrecy which has now been going on for ten years has placed a heavy strain on the constitution of American society. The state of mind which it has generated has distorted the right relationship among the various spheres which constitute the whole of American society. The right relationship among the three spheres of governmental powers has been subjected to a battering by the investigating committees. The equilibrium was certainly never completely upset. Powerful balancing forces have constantly been at work limiting the spread of disequilibrium in the structure of society. Moreover, the disrupters have not been interested in a total disruption of the pluralistic organization of society. The primitive and unelaborated nature of their obsession with secrecy, its unmasking and protection, has limited the range of damage to which they have aspired. If their passions had been formulated into a doctrine and a policy they might have infringed even more on the autonomy of the spheres. Nonetheless, injury has been done to American society, not just individual injustice but injury to the system as a whole. Any such monomania must always transgress the boundaries which protect separate areas of activity.

Every society is constructed of a set of spheres and systems: the domestic and kinship system, the political system, the economic system, the religious sphere, the cultural sphere, and the like. Different types of societies are characterized by the preponderance of one of the systems or spheres over the others. A theocracy, for example, is one in which the religious sphere and the ecclesiastical institutions and persons who administer them dominate the rest of the society. A plutocracy is one in which the wealthy, and especially businessmen, dominate the rest of the society, forcing it to conform to their standards. Political absolutism is the system in which politicians—hereditary, elected, acclaimed, or putschist — exercise uncontrolled power over the other spheres. The system of individualistic democracy or liberalism is characterized by an approximate balance among the spheres.

Liberalism is a system of pluralism.[1] It is a system of many centers of powers, many areas of privacy and a strong internal impulse towards the mutual adaptation of the spheres rather than of the dominance or the submission of any one to the others. Each sphere in the liberal society enjoys a partial autonomy and at the same time it influences and is influenced by the other spheres. It makes concessions to the needs of the other spheres—within the pattern of conduct of the individual and in the relations of institutions to one another. In the liberal society, church and state are separate but each respects the other and also exercises some influence on the other. In a liberal society, the economy is not run by the government and the government is not run by the owners or managers of the economy. Each respects the other, and exercises some influence over the other, while running itself in the light of its own inherent standards. If businessmen, *qua* businessmen, ran the government, we would have that caricature which Lenin thought described

---

1. All large-scale societies are inevitably pluralistic to some degree. The aspiration towards completely totalitarian control over all spheres of social life is unattainable, even by the most ruthless of elites. Incapacity on the one side, evasiveness, creativity and the necessity of improvisation on the other, introduce into totalitarian regimes, which would deny its validity, a good deal of pluralism. In such regimes, however, institutional autonomy is surreptitious and dangerous to those who practice it. It is constantly restricted and repressed. In liberal regimes, on the other hand, it is acknowledged and guaranteed and finds support in the legal system, the ethos and the distribution of legitimate power.

the modern "bourgeois" state.[2] In a liberal society, philosophers are not kings, the intellectuals do not rule any sphere except their own, nor do businessmen, politicians or priests govern intellectual life. In a liberal society, the intellectual sphere—the universities, the press, publishing houses, scientific academies and laboratories—must possess an extensive autonomy which is respected and facilitated by the elites of the political and economic spheres; the elites of the intellectual and cultural spheres must respect the autonomy of the political and economic spheres. Each must exercise a subtle influence over the other, each must feel a certain degree of respect and responsibility towards the other. They must be bound together not only by law and interest, but by a permeative sense of affinity and by a pluralistic system of values in which the dignity of the other realms of activity are accorded a high place.

An effectively working pluralistic system will feel no need for complete publicity. The mutual confidence of the elites of the different spheres and of the corporate bodies within the spheres renders unnecessary the perpetual disclosure of the private affairs of rivals and fellow citizens. A pluralistic society in a state of balance will not be preoccupied with secret conspiracies and it will not suspect whole sectors of the society of being willing to disclose secrets which are functionally necessary for the safety of the society. Privacy will accordingly be respected in such a regime. Moderate publicity will arouse no fears and privacy will not tend to turn into secrecy. An empathic sense of affinity with the rest of the society will make a fair degree of publicity acceptable and desirable. The feeling of being part of the larger society opens the mind to information about the rest of the society and arouses moderate curiosity about it.

---

2. Even though the Cabinet and the higher levels of the executive branch in the United States often draw on businessmen for important tasks, when they serve, they do not do so as businessmen but as government officials. The rule which requires the renunciation of conflicting interests is a testimony to this principle which requires that a man be capable of different loyalties in different situations.

One of the dangers to a liberal society is specialization to the point where understanding and sympathy for the other realms with which collaboration and a sense of affinity are necessary are obstructed. Men must find their jobs fascinating in order to do them creatively, and that condition cannot often be achieved without a long period of training. The skill and knowledge as well as the motive for doing a task up to a moderate level of efficiency can only be produced by specialization. Specialization in tasks and training is indispensable in a large-scale society, but its value is not unlimited. A society ruled by experts, specialized in their own fields and ignorant and indifferent of the rest, would be in a poor way to continue as a free society.

Specialization of task and training is often, however, characterized by an absence of concern for the fields outside the area of expertness. The specialist is an excellent caretaker of his own domain, but he is ordinarily not much concerned with the fate of what goes on outside. As long as the political ruling classes were recruited from the aristocracy or from the classes whose conduct was guided by an aristocratic ideal of life, there was an inevitable diffuseness in their range of interest and in their attitude towards their major tasks. The aristocrat was expected to act like a gentleman, to be interested in the administration of his estate, to be interested in sports and proficient in military skills, and he was naturally expected to take his place in the government of the country, locally and nationally.

The growth of specialized bureaucracies in the absolutist countries of the continent restricted the range of public activities of the aristocracy and the gentry. In Great Britain the amateur attitude of the ruling classes has persisted into the present century, despite the increase in the specialization of functions. In all countries the emergence of the modern university with its specialized training for the professions has contributed to the restriction of the scope of the political elite's relationship to the elites of the other spheres of society. Intra-elite relationships are impaired by specialization.

The amateur attitude is a necessity for freedom. It is obviously not the sole precondition. The amateur attitude is compatible with the utmost contempt for the mass of the population and a denial of their claims to dignity and justice. Amateurism is compatible with frivolousness, irresponsibility and incompetence to a degree great enough to destroy the social order, and it often threatens to turn into dilettantism. It is compatible with cruelty. It should not, therefore, be interpreted as an inevitable determinant of a regime of liberty. It is the underlying attitude of amateurism rather than functional amateurism that is so important to the liberal society. It is the disposition and sense of affinity with a variety of fields of action which is perfectly compatible with specialization but which appreciates the dignity of spheres other than that in which the individual is specialized. The amateur attitude towards other fields is perfectly compatible with reasonable specialization in one field, and without that combination modern liberal society would have a very hard time. The combination protects the relative autonomy of the spheres, acknowledging the value of the activities which make them up, providing the motives for the concern for one's own and respect for others. The politician who appreciates the military will not be a persecutor of the representatives of that profession. The politician who is a religious man will esteem the claims of the church to its own effective self-government. If he is a loyal son of his university he will be more respectful of the intellectual sphere. If he has experience in the administration of commerce or industry he is more likely to respect those who work in that sphere and to acknowledge their claims to self-government.

The institutional system of the pluralist society requires, then, that the elites of the various institutions should be attached to their institutions and to the values which are incorporated in them and which regulate them. The businessmen must enjoy business activity, be proud to be businessmen and feel responsible for the integrity of the business community in the face of all the other communities. The politician must enjoy politics, be willing to devote much of his best energy to it and to be convinced that politics is a fundamentally worthy human activity. The scientist certainly must be deeply convinced of the value of scientific truth and must be certain that it is one of the greatest human endeavors. The scholar, the journalist, the soldier, the administrator, the judge and the clergyman must all have similar sentiments about their own work and its position in the scale of values. This is not, however, sufficient. Even extreme specialization is adequate for the generation of such sentiments, but it does not offer what is required for all these separate activities to fit into a more or less articulated whole.

For that, the heritage of the amateur is needed. The elites must not only possess self-esteem; they must also esteem each other. The mutuality of esteem must be based on a sense of affinity, a sort of "consciousness of kind" among the elites of the various spheres so that they regard themselves together as parts of a unitary whole, within which differentiation exists and conflict is possible within the limits set by a loose and flexible solidarity. The amateur's appreciation of domains in which he is unspecialized is essential here.

The readiness to "live and let live" is essential to the free society in the relations among individuals and among corporate bodies, across as well as within the lines which separate the spheres. The respect for the right to privacy is required not only towards individuals, but towards corporate bodies and whole systems of corporate bodies. Trust in the benevolence or neutrality or justice of the other person and of the persons who live primarily in other spheres reduces the passion for publicity and damps down the fear of secrecy. It prevents the growth of the need for an intense and complete loyalty, ritualistically affirmed.

In their co-operation, too, the pluralistic principles of mutual respect are necessary. The genuineness, although not necessarily the correctness, of the judgment of the representatives of a given sphere, e.g., the scientific, must be mutually acknowledged if co-operation is to be effective. If one side cannot render its opinions frankly and openly without fear of imputation of ulterior and evil motives or of turning out in the long run of being on the wrong side and accordingly being morally wrong as well, the process of co-operation among peers cannot go on.[3]

The pluralistic society, with its respect for corporate privacy and the autonomy of the spheres and its requirement of the plural attachments of the sense of communal affinity, obviously has no place for a uniformizing and total loyalty to the symbols, standards and rulers of one particular sphere. Hyperpatriotism is an aberration in a pluralistic society. It is contrary to its nature and noxious to its functioning.

The patriotic loyalty of the pluralistic society is a loose affair, not worn on the sleeve; it is adduced only exceptionally as the standard of self-restraint in situations of potentially severe conflict. Ordinarily, the appreciation of the intrinsic values of the persons and activities across the dividing line is the more effective emollient of conflict. The pluralistic society keeps men's sentiments from flying outwards towards fixation on those remote objects which unsettle equanimity and disturb the pluralistic equilibrium. A well-working pluralistic society absorbs sufficient of the attention and affection of its members into a wide range of more proximate concerns—workshop, neighborhood, club, church, team, family, friends, trade union, school, etc. At least as important, it keeps down the need for a unification of all these loyalties into single loyalty. It confines the tendency, aroused and aggravated by crises, to fuse them all together into a single organism under a single standard. Not only does pluralism keep the loyalties from moving towards a single and remote object such as the nation, it limits the demand that the loyalties of others should be organized in that manner. When loyalties need not be total, then publicity need not be total since the recognition of the

---

3. The experience of Dr. Oppenheimer is, of course, the more extreme form in which this unbalance has come to light. It is indicative of the force of the pressure that an experienced unpolitical administrator, i.e., General Nichols, and a most civic-spirited citizen, Dr. Graham, should have yielded to it and searched for evidence of a loyalty-security defect in Dr. Oppenheimer's critical attitude towards the thermonuclear program.

right of loose and plural loyalty is also the recognition of the right to live in privacy.

This is the heart of pluralism. Without it there is no freedom.

II. The Rule of Law:
The Separation of Powers

The legal order which guarantees the pluralistic society is the rule of law—law made within the framework of a constitution, written or unwritten, by elected representatives, executed by a partially autonomous administrative staff and adjudicated by an independent judiciary.

The rule of law limits the powers of the government, both externally and internally. It is the limitation by law of the discretionary power of the executive over the other spheres of government and over the citizen; it is also the external and internal limitation of valid spheres of legislative action by constitution and custom, by tradition and morals. The rule of law is infringed when any one of the constituent authorities abdicates the functions appropriate to its partially autonomous sphere within the total system of authority or seeks so to expand it that it encroaches on the autonomy of another sphere. A bureaucracy which acts without reference to law infringes on the rule of law as much as a legislature which seeks to dominate the decisions of the judiciary. A legislative body which abandons its responsibilities to the populace which has elected it diverges from the rule of law as much as does a legislative which renounces its constitutional powers to the executive.

The rule of law rests at bottom on the belief widely and deeply diffused throughout the society that there is a sacred element in the law as such. The sacredness of the law is not confined to the law; it infuses the institutions through which it is made, applied, and adjudged. Like the pluralistic system as a whole, of which the rule of law is a part, it rests on the belief in the sacredness of a complex constellation of values, no one of which is always greatly superior to any other. Just as in the larger pluralistic system, each major and minor sphere has its own life, its own powers, and its own obligations of mutual adaptation, so in the rule of law each of the four sectors—the electorate, the legislature, the executive, and the judiciary—has its own autonomous realm and its obligations to the other realms which make up the system of the rule of law.

The rule of law is a delicately balanced affair and it must withstand battering from many sides. The populistic mentality, when it has full sway, denies the claims to autonomy of the legislative which it views as its mouthpiece, of the executive which it views as its instrument and of the judiciary which it views as the resistant custodian of a law which sets itself above the will of the people. Politicians are jealous of bureaucrats, whom they regard as rivals; bureaucrats with their greater detailed knowledge and their feeling of intimacy with the situation, sometimes dislike and bridle at the restrictions which the law places in the way of their doing what seems best.

In the United States the rule of law is deeply rooted in the interests of institutions and in a powerful tradition. Alongside of it, however, runs a current of thought and sentiment, a disposition towards ideological enthusiasm and political passions, which proclaim great crises and announce their disbelief in the capacities of ordinary institutions and their leaders to resolve them.

The American people are recurrently pulled in two directions: respect for the conventions of institutions and regard for the rights of others, and the opposite of these. There is a broad antinomian strand in the American people quite apart from the ordinary criminal element which even the best ordered of societies produces. There are times and areas of an exceptional irreverence and disrespect towards the law in the United States; it is widespread, if not often intense, in most sections of the population and it is perhaps more passive than active. The general attitude of the population towards nearly all municipal regulations, the not infrequent attempts to bribe officials, the only recently reduced tendency in certain regions to "take the law into one's own hands," the fact that in the 1930's hundreds of thousands of educated persons could without repugnance and without thought of the implications lend their support to a political organization which was committed in principle, even though at the time not in practice, to the unconstitutional revolutionary overthrow of the existing governmental and legal order, the toleration of small-scale urban civil wars during the 1920's and their intermittent revival since then, the whole fiasco of the observance of the Eighteenth Amendment—all of these instances and many others add up to the conclusion that, as far as one important prerequisite of the rule of law is concerned, American propensities are sometimes not quite all they should be.

Insistence, therefore, on the niceties of the rule of law is not likely to be an unchallenged response of Americans to crises. The disrespect for law is partly a function of the disrespect for the makers of the law, and that in its turn is reflected in the conduct of the makers of the law themselves. The populistic mentality and their own lack of disciplined self-respect impel them towards actions which conflict with the rule of law.

The loyalty-security program itself is significant of the abdication of Congress of its appropriate functions and its arrogation of functions which are not its own. Despite a decade of impassioned Congressional interest in loyalty and security, there is still no systematic set of statutes covering the entire field of loyalty and security. The statutes which do exist leave uncovered substantial parts of the field and they are uneven in their application. It could be said that the determination of disloyalty or unreliability in security matters is too subtle and delicate to be satisfactorily formulated in general laws, because specificity would impose rigidity, and vagueness would give rise to too many difficulties so that it would be best to grant adequate discretionary power to reliable administrative officials.[4] There would

---

4. Although it is now eight years since Executive Order 9835 was promulgated, the populistic auspices and atmosphere in which it was born have

be very good reasons to adopt such a policy, but this is not the policy which Congress has followed. While not taking the responsibility of formulating a clear set of rules in legislation it has been continuously active in the fields of loyalty and security, imposing particular security personnel on the executive departments, passing judgments on numerous particular decisions of security officials, causing cases once settled to be reopened, trying to force indictments of particular persons, pressing for punitive actions in individual cases, obtaining information which should be kept secret and which is even obtained under assurances of confidentiality and then disclosing it to the press, and doing countless other deeds which it is not the business of Congress to do. The Congressmen who have been most preoccupied with security did indeed lose their notion of the division of powers. At times, they acted as if they constituted a court for the trial of individuals, at others they have acted as an *ad hoc* and wilful administrative organ, especially in personnel matters. And even in the sphere which is properly their own they have gradually deformed and distorted their own functions.

The task of a legislative body is to legislate, to prepare itself for legislation by enquiry and discussion, and to scrutinize the results of its legislation in the action of the civil service. Legislation such as has come forth from the activities of the major investigating committees has been secondary in their intentions to their other functions. If their enquiries had resulted in better legislation then their wide-ranging curiosity could be better justified.

The greatest specific achievement of any of the investi-

---

left their mark. Congress has not attempted to promulgate into law a systematic and principled treatment of the security problem. The legislative treatment of the security problem has been *ad hoc* and fragmentary, being partially responses to specific requests by the executive branch and wild actions initiated in Congress for populistic motives. The amateur character of the board members and the nature of the permanent staff and the proceedings, have meant that no jurisprudence of security has developed. Although carried out on a grand scale, the program has not acquired the dignity of law. There has been no cumulative growth of knowledge, no cumulative clarification of standards. The judicial process has touched the security system only at a few accidental points.

gative committees has been the House Un-American Activities Committee's discovery that Alger Hiss had been a member of a Soviet spy ring in the 1930's and its forcing of his indictment for perjury. Hiss had ceased to be a government official and the events about which he was charged with perjury had occurred many years before. The surveillance of the state of security in the executive branch could not, therefore, be adduced to justify this enquiry into past history. The testimony of Miss Bentley and Mr. Chambers and the attempts to follow it up have been almost entirely historical. Compared with the excursions into events of more than ten years ago, attention to the present state of security in the civil service has been meagre. The greatest achievement of the Subcommittee on Internal Security of the Senate Judiciary Committee has been the destruction of the Institute of Pacific Relations and the indictment of Mr. Owen Lattimore, who had not been a government official for some years. It has not been claimed that Mr. Lattimore was still a Communist agent, nor that he has recently exercised influence in the government, nor even that he committed any actions which during the period of his alleged guilt were criminal. The Subcommittee enquiries in education brought about the dismissal, suspension, or some other deprivation of several score teachers in schools and colleges for their invocation of the Fifth Amendment when called to testify before the Subcommittee. Could it be said that such specific influence is part of the proper function of a legislative body?

The Senate Permanent Subcommittee on Investigations devoted a large part of its activities to the investigation of the personnel security system in private industry engaged on defense contracts. Senator McCarthy did not say that he was trying to improve the private administration of the defense department's security regulations; on the contrary, he said his main aim there was to obtain the dismissal of individuals and to bring about their indictment for perjury or contempt of Congress. The final explosion of Senator McCarthy's aspirations came in his search for the guilty party in the honorable discharge of an Army dentist alleged to be a Communist. Apart from the utter triviality and irrelevance of a dentist to the protection of military secrecy, the entire disturbance arose out of the pursuit of particular individuals rather than a concern for the working of the security system.

Thus one of the major consequences of the investigative committees' work has been the punishment of individuals through dismissal from private or public employment, the citation, indictment, and conviction for contempt of Congress, and the obstruction of the subsequent careers of the persons so punished.

It is also an important task of a legislative body to educate public opinion by its enquiries and debates. In the United States the educative function of Congressional debate has long been in suspension. The possibility of publicity without the challenge and without the competition of debate has put Congress as a forum into the shadows. It would be difficult to say that such one-sided campaigns as the investigative committees have carried on with their preoccupation with the pursuit of individuals and the assertion of the broadest generalities about conspiratorial networks have made the American people more realistic in understanding the nature of the threat of Communism. What the committees have perhaps done is to increase the distrust in which government is held—by those who accept the committees' views, for being permeated by conspirators, and by those who do not, for being dominated by unscrupulous and fanatical demagogues. If this is so, then respect for the laws made and executed by such a government must be diminished and the rule of law weakened. The result is on the one side to strengthen populism and on the other to weaken civility and to cause excessive withdrawal into privacy, which is often a privacy full of resentment and bitterness towards the politicial sphere.

In their relations with the executive departments, the investigating committees repeatedly broke through the separation of powers. Although this had been going on ever since the investigating committees began their work, it only became widely noticed during the last phase of Senator McCarthy's ascendancy. His summons to officials of the executive branch to disregard their obligations to their superiors and to turn over to him any evidence they encountered of inadequacies in the administration of loyalty and security became one of the issues in the censure hearings. The Select Committee did not, however, pass judgment on his attempt and temporary success at controlling the State Department policy for the Voice of America and the United States Information Service. Nor did it pass judgment on his action to force an end to trade with Communist countries.

Through his egregious aides he gained temporary control over the libraries of the Information Service. For a time he controlled the Voice of America. He intruded into specific decisions on personnel, compelling the dismissal, suspension, or resignation of Theodore Kaghan, Reed Harris and numerous others in the State Department and the Voice of America, the U.S. Information Service, the Army Signal Center at Fort Monmouth and in many private firms.

In their relations with the Department of Justice the investigating committees have functioned as pressure groups and competitors. The irrational and vindictive pursuit of the Communist agent, Gerhard Eisler, who was being held for deportation and who "deported" himself by escaping on the Polish ship Batory in the spring of 1949, was characteristic of the efforts of the Department to avoid the shadow of criticism that they were not doing everything in their power to make Communists as miserable as possible.

The Lorwin case was perhaps the best illustration of the degenerative influence of the legislative agitation about loyalty and security. The case was a direct outgrowth of Senator McCarthy's demands for action against individuals. Mr. Lorwin had been cleared by the Loyalty Board of the State Department after two very thorough examinations. Nonetheless, since concessions had to be made to Senator McCarthy's demand that action be taken against the "card-carrying" members of the Communist Party whom he alleged to be working in the State Department, the Department of Justice asked the grand jury to indict Mr. Lorwin. So powerful was the pressure to please McCarthy, that the Department of Justice allowed deliberate misrepresentations to be made to the grand jury by its own lawyer in order to obtain the indictment. The grand jury was deliberately misinformed to the effect that Mr. Lorwin would claim the immunity of the Fifth Amendment and would refuse to testify about his convictions and affiliations. By this falsification, the Department of Justice managed to exclude Mr. Lorwin from the grand jury hearings and thus succeeded in obtaining the indictment. Meanwhile it was perfectly evident to the Department that Mr. Lorwin was willing to testify at great length about his convictions and affiliations. In fact, when the case came to be heard in the Federal District Court, the Department withdrew the case because the spurious nature of its case was so obvious that it felt that it would have no chance of success.

That the decision to withdraw the case was not a product of a respect for the legal rights of the defendant was evident in the Department's conduct in the court. In order to avoid exposure of its shady work, the Department was refusing to obey the orders of the court. Yet when the case by its own admission collapsed, the Department never had the courage to have the indictment withdrawn. From its inception to its inglorious culmination, the Lorwin case was a demonstration of the way in which the demagogy of secrecy and conspiracy was affecting the executive branch, and particularly that department with the greatest responsibility to prevent justice from becoming lynch law.[5]

The general disorder into which the division of labor among the three spheres of government has been thrown

---

5. Although the lawyer who handled the case was dismissed from his post, it must not be thought that his conduct was simply a product of personal incompetence or dishonesty. He would not have acted as he did had he not felt that he had to bring in an indictment and a conviction and if he had not believed that his superiors wished him to use whatever dishonorable means were necessary or would at least tolerate his action as long as he was successful in obtaining the imprisonment of an innocent person.

by the uproar of the committees is manifest in other aspects of the conduct of the Department of Justice. The Attorney General himself, anxious that the administration should not lose the political advantage which appeared to come from exploiting the fear of subversion presumed to exist in the country as a whole, entered into the competition with the investigating committees. It could have been only considerations of party advantages of a sort which are problematic enough when Congressmen are moved by them, which led the Attorney General to renew the old charges against the late Harry D. White and to imply that the former President Truman had been indifferent to the reports of White's collusion in espionage. Partly to sidestep the force of Congressional anger about subversion and to gratify their desire for victims of the fear of espionage, and partly to take the political initiative from Congress and to give it back to the executive, the Attorney General sallied forth. The burden of his attack had nothing to do with the then present state of security in the country. The events referred to, as in most of the agitation about secrecy, had occurred years before and even if they were as alleged, they contributed nothing to public enlightenment about present threats to information-security or to the efficient safeguarding of important secrets.

The antipathetic attitude of the Department of Justice towards the rule of law—an attitude engendered by the vindictive demand for victims by the more vigorous Congressional agitators about subversion and the Department's amalgam of submission and competition — appears again in the Lattimore case. Refusing to be deprived of its quarry, the Department sought to convict Mr. Lattimore of perjury concerning sentiments which are almost impossible to define, which were not criminal when they were allegedly thought, and which in any case occurred years ago. When Judge Youngdahl, acting within his prerogatives, threw out several of the charges and impugned others and was partially sustained by a higher court, the U.S. Attorney, Mr. Rover, tried to bludgeon Judge Youngdahl into disqualifying himself. This is as far as anyone within the Federal Government has dared to go in recent years to intrude on the autonomy of the judiciary and it can only be attributed to the insistence of the Congressional huntsmen of conspiracy and custodians of secrecy.

The deterioration of the rule of law under the impact of a nervous populism which is concerned with homogeneity of attitude is evident in the indictment which the Department of Justice brought against Mr. Lattimore. His misdeeds—apart from the alleged perjury of his denial—include attitudes or subjective states of an extraordinary imprecision. He is said to have been a "sympathizer," he is said to have been a "follower of the Communistic line," to have been a "promoter of Communist interests." It is not just technically poor work in the preparation of the indictment which is revealed here, nor is it simply desperation to find some charges by which Mr. Lattimore can be convicted. Both these factors are probably operative, but at least as important is the populistic mentality which disregards the law and seeks to punish those who have the wrong *dispositions.*

The State Department has naturally been the object of the campaign against subversion. How could populistic demagogues do other than accuse that stronghold of alleged xenophilia, internationalism, Eastern seaboard culture, and excessive refinement, of conspiracy and the disclosure of secrets? Although the fundamental lines of American foreign, economic, diplomatic, and military policy have not been determined by the investigators, they have influenced its personnel, their methods and their outlook. To take only the most obvious example, the appointment of Mr. Scott McLeod as Chief Security and Personnel Officer of the State Department—a man of limited qualifications for such an extraordinarily responsible post—was the acknowledgment by the State Department of the right of the Congressional huntsmen of subversion and espionage to set their own watchdog in the very midst of the Department. The successive re-examinations of the security clearance of Mr. John P. Davies, its ultimate withdrawal and Mr. Davies' dismissal, is another instance of the way in which the investigating agencies have succeeded in moving away from their legitimate task of presenting a broad picture made up of truthful details and constructive and realistic legislative proposals based on these, and gone over towards guerilla administration. The State Department has been forced to undertake many trivial actions which were ill-advised, out of deference to Congress' insistence in hunting down the disloyal. The action of the American delegates to the United Nations, and the United States ambassadors in Latin America in trying to assemble support for American resistance to the Administrative Tribunal's compensation award to the eleven American employees of the United Nations who had refused to testify before Congressional investigating committees was certainly generated by fear of Congressional reprisals. On a more important plane, the long rigidity of American policy towards the Soviet Union and the sterility of the State Department in devising a more differentiated and imaginative policy are the fruits of the Congressional fear of being overcome by the Communist conspiracy.

In its passport and visa policies, the State Department has shown the same rigidity born of intimidation by the Congressional watchers over loyalty and secrecy. It is true that the visa provisions of the Immigration and Nationality Act are themselves a monument to the unrealistic fear of the conspiratorial penetration into our secrets. But within the law, United States consuls have played for safety and left their meagre discretionary power unused for fear of having to answer before a Congressional investigating committee which might charge them with having knowingly admitted a particular Communist. In consequence, in a great number of cases, visas have been refused or action has been so long delayed as to be equivalent to refusal. The McCarran-Walter Act, although cumbersome, has been administered worse than the law itself requires. Nor could its extraordinarily rigid administration be accounted for by the fact that the knowledge of foreign political movements and ideologies is not likely to be found in the equipment of a consular officer. The real source of the difficulty lies in the Congressional spirit which watches over the law.

The excitement engendered by the scent of a secret and the absence of any sense of boundaries dividing institutional jurisdictions is seen in the Congressional investigating committees' methods of investigation. While the FBI is always praised most highly by these bodies, their love and enthusiasm for the public penetration of the enemies' secrets is so great that they cannot resist the temptation to feature undercover agents such as are employed by the FBI. The value of such agents in counterespionage lies in their being kept out of publicity. The investigating committees are not, however, content to allow anything they touch to remain closed to publicity. Hence, in their expansiveness, they have even entered into the sphere of the Federal Bureau of Investigation, which alone of government agencies they adore, tempting some of their undercover informers to come to the investigating committees' hearings as witnesses and offering them the pleasures of publicity.

Like other politicians, they regard the possession of a secret as an occasion to boast—and since boasting would be empty without the disclosure of the secret, the investigating committees which are consecrated to the coercive enforcement of government secrecy are themselves from time to time the sources of disclosures.

The distorted image which the investigating committees have of themselves and their eagerness to take over the role of the executive in areas in which they are active is vividly illustrated by the great file of names of individuals tainted with conspiracy maintained by the House Committee on Un-American Activities. This great file, indiscriminately crowded with false, vague, half-true, and completely true information, covers a multitude of persons. It is the kind of file which a counterespionage organization would keep, but is scarcely appropriate to a body concerned with the formulation of a general picture of the situation and the proposal of improved legislation. Such a file can only be the product of phantasies of including the executive branch as part of itself.

The erosion of institutional boundaries by the passion of loyalty is to be seen not only in the relations between the three sectors of government, but also in the conceptions governing the executive branch itself. A gigantic corporate body like the executive branch of the federal government must necessarily consist of many quasi-autonomous departments and agencies, divisions, branches, etc., whose boundary lines and jurisdictions are more or less clearly defined. The conception of moral or ideological infection is the enemy of the conception of definite jurisdiction. The antinomy appears in the problem of sensitive and non-sensitive positions. Nominally the loyalty-security program provides for the distinction between sensitive and non-sensitive positions. Whereas the British security system, which, whatever its deficiencies, is a security and not a loyalty system, provides for transfers of Communists to non-sensitive positions, Mr. Seth Richardson who was in charge of the Federal program said, ". . . it would be extremely difficult, if not impossible, to evolve any formula for distinguishing non-sensitive from sensitive agencies. The numerous transfers of employees, the changes in their duties, the size of government departments, and the number of activities involved, would make the non-sensitive employee of one day the sensitive employee of the next. Moreover, the presence in even a non-sensitive government organization of a disaffected non-sensitive employee, might, through contact and association, lead to the infection of loyal and possibly sensitive employees. One bad apple may ultimately infect the whole barrel!"[6]

The same conception of the internal boundarylessness of the executive branch appeared in the Gray Board Report on Dr. Oppenheimer, where it was said that Dr. Oppenheimer's appointment as a consultant could not simply be

---

6. *Columbia Law Review* (1952), 51, p. 553.

terminated without formally and separately revoking his
security clearance, since then other government departments would continue to employ his services—as if the
Atomic Energy Commission were responsible for the security programs of all other government departments.

There are, of course, obvious limits to the extent in a
great organization all boundaries can be swept away and
to which a legislative body, for example, can intrude into
and attempt to supersede an executive body. As regards
continuous executive action, it is impossible for it to accomplish anything significant. It is, however, very possible,
by commando-like operations and the threat of painful
sanctions, to set policy here or there in a given direction,
to bring about the dismissal of some officials, and to intimi-
date others into carrying out the "line" which is suggested
by its enquiries and criticisms. More importantly, the legislative enquiry and tirade can constrict day-to-day policy-
making and force it to avoid certain paths of action. The
specific efforts to supplant the executive, although repre-
hensible, have, on the whole, been inconsequential.[7] It is
by its permeative or effluvial influence on the executive
branch that the investigating committees have exercised
a notable influence. Particularly in sections of the government which have been subject to repeated attacks, the result
is not so much the execution of the will of the investigating

---

7. The Eisenhower administration repeatedly made efforts to conciliate
the Congressional bullies when they sought to usurp the executive function,
e.g.: when Mr. Stassen rebuffed McCarthy for interfering in the Greek
shipping affair, Vice-President Nixon persuaded him to take a more conciliatory line; when Mr. Dulles reinstated Mr. McLeod to the powers which
had been withdrawn from him and when Mr. Corsi's appointment was
rescinded; when, following President Eisenhower's criticism of book burning,
the White House at McCarthy's suggestion refused to allow the speech to
be broadcast over the Voice of America; when the Department of Justice
took no action on the Senate's reports on Senator McCarthy's financial
affairs and on irregularities in the Maryland elections; when Robert E. Lee,
who was involved in the Maryland election's irregularities, was appointed
to the Federal Communications Commission; and when Secretary Stevens
retreated before McCarthy's offensive. Many other instances could be added
of efforts by the administration to avoid conflict over the invasion of its
jurisdiction.

committee as the avoidance of its wrath by anxious caution or apathetic and fearful conformity.

The impact of the investigative committee of the legislative branch moves through indirect channels. It reaches the press and Congressional colleagues and then, by heating the atmosphere, it reaches into the executive branch. A few personalities then become the symbols of the attack, but they are not the attackers. The attack is carried out along a broader front and is less easily located. Its amorphousness makes it even more effective in penetrating the executive sphere. The agitation about secrecy, subversion, and espionage has disturbed the balance of autonomy and responsibility in the relationship of the spheres within the government,[8] and in the relations of the government to the

---

8. A passage in the Report of the Select Committee of the Senate which proposed the censure of Senator McCarthy, reasserted the nice sense of tact, the combination of independence and trust necessary for the working of the separation of powers. Discussing the right of Congress to executive branch documents, it expressed the attitude which has been in constant conflict with the populistic erosion of boundaries and which is now reassuming a more positive form after years of mounting adversity. It said: "The Executive Branch is, initially, particularly charged with enquiry into and suppression of the insidious infiltration of subversives into its own departments and agencies; this responsibility is a delicate and necessarily confidential one because it involves the clearing of loyal personnel as well as the identification and elimination of disloyal employees. It also involves techniques of investigation which must be kept secret to be effective. . . .

". . . if this system . . . were to be presented to the Congress as an Iron Curtain denying to properly authorized agencies or persons (in which the Congress and its committees are to be placed first) any right of access, a situation would be presented against which this committee would protest with all its power as other committees have protested in the past. This we would regard as a challenge to the co-equal powers of the legislative branch.

"If on the other hand, the executive has recognized the prerogatives of the Congress . . . to be informed of classified material or information by orderly and formal application to responsible heads of departments or to the Presidential Office itself, then the Committee believes another problem of constitutional government may be presented and that the Senate itself would be the first to respect the necessary right of the Executive to protect its special functions so long as the equally important powers of the Legislative branch are not unduly impeded thereby.

"We would be of the view that for the Executive department, even the President himself, to deny to properly constituted committee or subcommittee of the Senate, or any Senator operating with the authority in the matter, facts involving wrongdoings in any Executive department, that

other spheres. In the course of this agitation, the criterion of hyperloyalty has come to be a postulate of much governmental action in the recruitment of personnel and in the selection among alternative policies. Standards of ideological perfection, of hyperpatriotism, diffuse outward as the government extends the range of its activities and introduces and imposes these criteria on all it meets.

---

might well offer a proper ground for challenging such a decision on the broadest and soundest constitutional grounds. By the same token, a failure of the Congress or any member to adapt itself or himself to reasonable regulation by the President or his authorized department heads (for example, the Departments of Defense or the Federal Bureau of Investigation) with respect to matters involving national security, might readily expose the Congress to an equally sound criticism."

CHAPTER 7

THE AUTONOMY OF SCIENCE

I. The Tradition

THERE IS AN INNER AFFINITY between science and the pluralistic society. The conduct of scientific research requires a pattern of relationships among scientists which is the prototype of the free society. In microcosm, the scientific community mirrors the larger free society. The internal freedom of the scientific community requires also a freedom from external control. The internal freedom of the scientific community requires the autonomy of science, and whatever may be the relationship among the other spheres of a society, their relationship to the scientific community must be pluralistic.

Quite independently of modern individualistic liberalism, the tradition of the free community of science has grown up. The chief elements in this tradition are internal publicity of the results and procedures of scientific research and free admission to the profession of science on the basis of the qualifications necessary for the conduct of scientific research.

The community of science is built around the free communication of ideas among a relatively small number of intellectually interested and qualified persons whose judgment is recognized to be a measure of validity, and whose approbation gives confidence in the truthfulness of discoveries and in the fruitfulness of the paths traversed. This tradition is part of the fundamental constitution of science. Without it science could not exist. Science is not a collection of results of individual investigators who happen to have been working on the same subjects at more or less the same time. Science is the product of a very informal community of many scientists working on similar or related problems—matching their own results with one another's or using them as the point of departure for their own investigations. The communication of scientists takes place through publication in scientific journals, through the distribution of offprints, through private correspondence and conversation. This has been harshly misunderstood by the custodians of loyalty and security.

This system of communication is not a tradition in the sense that it is an outworn vestige to which people are irrationally attached just because they have been attached to it in the past. It is a tradition which has grown out of the work itself, as a necessary part of it and as an indispensable condition of its continuation. Without free discussion and the possibility of contact with ideas different from his own, a scientist can seldom discover new implications in his own ideas. It is not that someone else tells him what his ideas imply—although this often happens, and with great benefit—nor does he simply add the other scientist's insight to his own. Rather, contact with the other scientist's train of thought sets his own going in directions in which it might not have gone by itself. In this way discoveries are made, science grows, and mankind gains in stature and in welfare.

The decisive fact is that in the autonomous scientific community, decisions as to truth and falsity, as to feasibility, and appropriateness, are made by scientists in the light of standards which their own best judgment recommends. These standards are inherited in the scientific tradition. They are the product of the reflection, observation, and genius of the best minds of several centries; they undergo continual and gradual revision, clarification and improvement in accordance with the judgment of scientists who respect their own tradition and yet move freely, critically and creatively within it.

Fundamentally, the autonomy of science or of any field of activity is infringed on when its practitioners are required to conform with an ideal of ideological perfection, to an ideal which requires in the individual's past, present, and probable future conduct and associations a complete conformity with an ideal of the perfect American—such as has been implicit in many decisions of American security officers.

The standard of truth in science has nothing to do with the criteria of political success or of political loyalty. A scientific proposition is true or false in accordance with the standards which are appropriate to scientific judgment. Whether a scientific proposition is true or false depends not at all on whether the person who asserts it is a loyal American, a loyal Russian, a disloyal American, or a politically indifferent Frenchman or Pole. A member of the Communist Party might be a poor scientist, but the determination as to whether he is a poor scientist can be made only by qualified scientists who would not consider his Communist affiliation in arriving at their judgment.

The autonomy of science is infringed on when scientists who are qualified by their training, personal qualities and intellectual gifts, as assessed by their peers and seniors, are prevented for extra-scientific reasons from working on problems on which research is possible and for which resources are available. It is infringed on when scientists are unable to discuss, publish, or circulate their work to other scientists interested in the same or related problems. It is infringed on when scientists are unable to leave their country or to enter another country to attend a scientific congress because the government in the country from which they come or to which they wish to go is concerned about their ideological adequacy. It is infringed on when talented young scientists are refused grants which are otherwise available and for which they are otherwise qualified, or when older and well-established scientists are refused research grants for which their achievements and reputation qualify them because their ideological disposition is adjudged to be unsatisfactory.

The introduction of loyalty criteria for the Fellows of the Atomic Energy Commission or for recipients of grants of the U.S. Public Health Service to conduct research on subjects having nothing to do with weapons or military security has been such an infringement. It has likewise been an infringement when a few universities have been reluctant to employ scientists who have been unable to obtain security clearance for work on classified subjects because the universities have hoped to obtain subsequently government contracts which require that all scientists on the projects have security clearance. (The development of similar policies in industrial firms employing scientists and hoping to obtain defense contracts also constitute infringements of the autonomy of economic life.)

The autonomy of science is further infringed by the McCarran-Walter Act and the rigid application of the visa provisions by consular officials and the Visa Division of the State Department when they deny visas to scientists who wish to enter the United States to attend public scientific congresses or to do unclassified research at American universities. The fact that these scientists in some of the many instances, but by no means all, had once been connected or were still peripherally connected with groups now classified as Communist or Communist-front organizations in the United States has not rendered the infringement of autonomy any less real or effective. The withholding of passports from American scientists by the State Department is no less an infringement on the autonomy of science, although fortunately it has been less frequent than the refusal of visas.

These are simple, superficial instances of the intrusion. It is no less an infringement of the autonomy of science when political criteria are self-imposed. When those who are charged with the maintenance of the autonomy of their sphere adopt criteria which emanate from another sphere, they are to that extent renouncing their independence.

When the American Council of Learned Societies, which has in its charge the furtherance of humanistic studies, is forced into a position where it defends itself by pointing to its work on dictionaries, which if they could obtain additional financial support, would allow the United States to compete more effectively with the Soviet Union, the professors of humanistic studies have ceased to see their subjects as intrinsically, autonomously valuable and have taken over the standards of another sphere. Throughout American academic life, there has emerged a tendency to legitimate scientific and scholarly activities on utilitarian grounds—on grounds of aiding the conduct of the Cold War, of contributing to material well-being, etc. It is not that these goals are unworthy or that scientific and scholarly studies should not aid in their realization. The principle of partial autonomy requires consideration for the goals of the other spheres and for the maintenance of the entire society as well. But when there is never an argument given regarding the intrinsic value of the activity there is something wrong. Either the administrators of the learned lack the necessary self-esteem, or they feel so unappreciated by their society that they think they cannot aver their real sentiments about the true value of their intellectual activities.[1]

The tradition of an autonomous community of scientists, regulating their own culture, determining what is true and what is false by observation and analysis freely made and freely communicated, entails a system of publicity far from the populistic tradition of publicity, but in America it has been able, under favorable circumstances, to coexist with and even gain encouragement and sustenance from it. Persons brought up in the culture in which publicity is accepted have felt no strain of contradiction with the world of science. They came indeed to think that the complete freedom of criticism of all and everything and the lack of respect for authority made America more harmonious with science than other, more hierarchical countries. To those who grew up in the culture of the scientific community, the widespread practice of publicity seemed—insofar as they concerned

---

1. Nowhere is this tendency more visible than in the social sciences. Either out of a desire to obtain funds not otherwise available or because the value of their enquiries in the discovery of truth is less appealing to them, social scientists greatly overstate the immediate practical value of their studies and do less than justice to their potential value in the disinterested search for truth. This cannot be attributed to the preoccupation with secrecy and conspiracy, but it is closely related to the more basic populistic strain in American culture.

themselves at all with what went on outside science—to be no more than right.

There was, however, a point at which the two traditions diverged. Ever since the last decade of the nineteenth century there have been explosions of populistic hostility against big business, or against government, or against the intellectuals. It has not been by any means continuous or universal, but in each of the past seven decades there has been a flurry of excitement against the people's enemies. The battle was fought "on behalf of the people" by politicians. It was there that the autonomy of science, necessary to its existence, was interpreted as aloofness and a feeling of superiority, the interest in pure science derided as self-indulgence and a sign of inadequate appreciation of the needs of the people. The ivory tower was assailed as morally suspect.

Science, particularly science which bears fruit in technology and in public health, is much appreciated in the United States, and even the pure scientist has rarely been regarded as worse than a harmless eccentric and at best as a new priesthood and the parent of technology and material well-being. But wherever there is a residue of traditionalism there is also a lurking distress about science as the critic of inherited beliefs. Fundamentalism came into existence in America as a theological movement which sought to repulse the movement of the scientific attitude towards traditional religion. Its major engagement with modern science was at Dayton, Tennessee, and it cannot be said that the Scopes trial had any significant consequences for the development of American science. American science was carried on in the great universities with sufficient self-esteem and attachment to the traditions of intellectual freedom, and the physical and biological research encountered no obstacles.[2] The

---

2. The path of the social sciences, too, was quite unobstructed in the great universities, although those subjects have not ceased to be under intermittent attack from the outside, during the present century. It should be noted that the attackers almost always alleged that they acted in defense of traditional institutions and moral beliefs, that research was scarcely

Scopes trial was of interest only as a notification to the larger world of a tense undercurrent of distrust towards science and scientists.

II. *Science, Politics, and Security*

For most of the first half of the present century, science lived as it always had in the past, largely unto itself. The increasing industrial application of science did not cause any worry because industrial science was on the whole applied science and the small amount of industrial secrecy involved was of no consequence for the life of the scientific community and for the ethos of scientists. Publicity within the community of science was unhampered. It was only when governments decided that science was useful and even entirely crucial to military strength and to national survival that the trouble began. On the one hand, science began to benefit from a largesse which hitherto the greatest private patrons, local and state government bodies, and philanthropic and educational foundations could never afford. On the other hand, it began to find itself working under rather embarrassing and constricting circumstances.

The Second World War brought scientists into a new realm, bounded and criss-crossed by secrecy and compartmentalization. During the war scientists chaffed at the restraints, complained to one another, and accumulated much distress about the restrictions imposed by the security system. They undoubtedly infringed on the lesser security rules of compartmentalization, not because they were gossips or busybodies, but because they had to do so in order to get their work done. They did not challenge the principle of security against the passage of information into the hands of agents of enemy or potentially hostile powers, and they even respected this principle when the foreign power was a military ally at the time. Dr. Oppenheimer's action re-

---

attacked at all, teaching somewhat more and especially in the lesser colleges and state universities, and that the external political activity of social scientists was the most frequent target.

garding Mr. Chevalier is probably only one of many instances in which scientists, although not regarding the subordinate details of the security system as sacred, respected the fundamental principle and refused to disclose classified information to an outsider. As far as we know, the war ended without a serious breach in security by any American scientist. It also ended with military nerves frayed by the wilfulness of scientists, their slipshodness with respect to the details of military security, their individuality and waywardness.

The end of the war brought no remission for American science. The rapid discovery of the expansionist tendency of Soviet policy forced the United States government to remain as active in the field of science as it had been during the war. The government has remained far and away the chief source of funds for scientific research. Normal caution would have dictated an alert program of information and personnel security since a substantial fraction of the research was directly relevant to military technology, and a security system alone would have been difficult enough. The situation was sorely aggravated, however, by the attraction which science and scientists exercised for persons preoccupied with *maximal loyalty* and obsessed simultaneously by secrecy and publicity.

The fundamentalist hostility towards science, the populist preoccupation with conspiracy and its dislike of rarified intellectual interests, had hitherto been without great weight in the life of the scientific community. They became more weighty only when events over which they had no influence presented secrecy and conspiracy as a more realistic problem. Their own imaginations became inflamed and they communicated some of their own agitation to those who had to deal with secrecy and conspiracy as practical problems.

The atomic bomb and the subsequent discussion of the secret as the source of American strength made some sectors of American opinion feel that their survival lay in the hands of university scientists, a species which had not previously ranked very high in their esteem. The arrest of Dr. Alan Nunn May and the disclosure of the atomic energy espionage ring in Canada under the control of Soviet diplomatic officials, the testimony of Miss Bentley and Mr. Chambers, the Hiss and Coplon trials, Fuchs and then Pontecorvo, and the Rosenbergs, were evidence of the vigor of Soviet espionage and of the dangers which it brought for the retention of secret scientific knowledge on which our national security in part depended. It also encouraged a belief that scientists were not reliable. What was more natural than for those already inclined to be suspicious to begin with to suspect the scientists of faltering loyalty and of inadequate reliability in matters of security? After all, a few eminent scientists had, before the war, lent their names to the proclamations of Communist fellow-travelling organizations; a small number of younger scientists had been members of the Communist Party or had expressed sympathy with it before, during, and even after the war; and one scientist was known to have spent an evening with a Soviet consular official.

Thus, among those figures in the legislative branch who arrogated to themselves the protection of the security system, scientists tended to fall under a blanket of suspicion. Their dislike for the security system arising from their devotion to the free tradition of science was mistaken for a hostility towards the security system arising from political considerations and, more particularly, from attachment to subversive political beliefs and movements. Political sympathies of the prewar period, often the sympathies of youthful enthusiasm and of the naiveté of a first discovery of the world's problems, were taken as valid evidence of present unreliability in security matters.

Scientists have been expected to prove themselves beyond others because they bear a mark of original sin. They are intellectuals and very different from the ordinary back-slapping, vigorous, go-ahead sorts of men. A very important administrator of scientists, who is himself no scientist, said not many years ago about a very important scientist X who had annoyed him greatly, something like: "X is abnormal. If only he had been interested in sports when he was a boy, just like Y." (Y too is an extremely eminent scientist who since this general exculpation has lost his security clearance.)

This might explain the distrust. The demand for perfection in conduct, associations, and loyalty has perhaps another source. The scientist, like the bureaucrat, is a challenge to the legislator while nominally his subordinate. His recondite knowledge gives him the upper hand. The scientists are able to obtain immense sums of money to discover ways of protecting the country. The politician cannot reasonably be expected to possess the knowledge necessary for adequate supervision of the scientist's work, and yet he feels a responsibility for doing so. Where the results of their work cannot be checked in detail, and where indeed the executive branch discourages it, there is a corresponding increase in the fervor to check on their qualities, on their attitudes, and above all on their loyalty.

Party because what they do is so important to the national military security, partly, too, because although they have an enormous responsibility conferred on them, they are not trusted, scientists (and higher civil servants) have come to bear the brunt of the loyalty-security measures. There can be no doubt that scientists are more scrutinized, picked over, and controlled by the loyalty-security system than any other profession or occupation in the United States.

It is practically impossible to discover with any accuracy just how many scientists who are subject to the system have fallen afoul of it. An official of the Federation of American Scientists, given to moderation in his judgments, estimates very tentatively that somewhere in the neighborhood of a thousand qualified scientists have encountered security difficulties. Few of these have been in the same class of scientific eminence as Dr. Oppenheimer, Dr. Pauling, Dr. Condon, or Dr. Peters, but they have been highly trained and qualified scientists, well capable of contributing much to knowledge and the national welfare.

At least one hundred and probably several hundred foreign scientists, most of them of high distinction and many of the greatest eminence, have been prevented from coming into the United States to participate in discussions with their American colleagues, to present papers at scientific congresses and to conduct non-secret research in American laboratories.

Like most Americans brought up in the tradition of a loose pluralistic society and not given to worrying much about the symbols of the whole society, American scientists rallied without reservations to the war effort. The great achievements of the scientists on behalf of the nation are very well known, especially to those who most harry them. No single scientist has been shown to be a spy. None of the famous scientist spies—Fuchs, Nunn May and Pontecorvo—were American; none of the American spies—Greenglass, Sobel, Gold or Rosenberg—were higher than technicians or engineers. The few American minor scientists who were alleged to be involved in espionage have never been shown to have been spies.

No professionals have been asked to sacrifice so much of their own tradition as the scientists. The freedom of publication and discussion is absolutely central to the tradition of science. Yet for about a dozen years, large numbers of American scientists have been required to forego both these necessities on behalf of "compartmentalization" and "classification." They have suffered from misunderstanding, often well-intentioned, but sometimes suspicious, by their military supervisors and their security officers, who have not always understood their nature and their needs. They have done many things which have been foreign to the tradition of free science. On the whole, they have done so without more than a complaint which has accepted the postulates of the system about which they complained.

No profession in a position so invested with crucial knowledge has maintained its trust so well. No other profession has been so suspected by the fanatics of secrecy and those who fall victim to their agitation;[3] none has been more insulted by the ideologists of hyperpatriotism than scientists.

III. The Impact on Science

What has been the effect of the security-loyalty measures? The effect on science as such is difficult to assess. It is impossible even for a scientist of genius to assess a lost opportunity of which he was unaware. The freedom of science is so important to its progress just because it allows the accidental to occur. Discovery of scientific truth is too unpredictable to allow anyone to say exactly what has been lost to American science through the unnecessary restriction of communication and the distraction and harassment generated by a security system made more extreme than realism requires, out of an obsession with loyalty. A small number of senior scientists and some outstanding younger scientists have apparently refused to work in fields dominated by the security procedures. A large number have been prevented from working in these fields, and an even larger group, consisting mainly of younger men of high quality, who are both cleared and willing to work under security procedures, feel constricted in working under what they consider conditions of unjustifiable discrimination, diminution of their freedom, and lack of esteem for the dignity of science.

There has never been any likelihood of anything remotely approximating a wholesale exodus or a general strike or a widespread boycott of scientists against the government. There is, however, a vague and growing feeling among some of the most distinguished scientists of the older generation, and more commonly in the younger generation, that they are serving masters who have no sense of the tasks scientists

---

3. A high official of the United States embassy in London once shouted in reply to a request for help in obtaining a visit for a famous British scientist and philosopher, well known for his anti-Communism, "Oh, that's it! He's a scientist. We've had some experience with them. We've been bitten by them."

and the country as a whole are facing, and who are often utterly inaccessible to reason. There is a growing feeling that life in the university is better than life in a government laboratory and that even within a university, work on unclassified projects is better than work on classified subjects. Scientists appreciate the financial generosity of government departments and they appreciate, too, the efforts of the administrators and military men with whom they have to deal to facilitate their work and to spare them some of the ignominies which otherwise might await them. It is not so much the technically necessary secrecy which disturbs them —there are very few scientists and none of serious stature who deny the need for some system of security—as it is the atmosphere which has been generated. One of the most respected American scientists, Professor Hans Bethe, no radical and no enemy of security, has said, "Perhaps the greatest impediment to the scientist . . . is the political climate of the country. . . . We sense a distrust of scientists and of intellectuals in general, in Washington and some newspapers and among many radio commentators. Concern about the future development of this trend is perhaps the greatest outside influence which hinders the effective work of scientists."

Nor is this view confined to scientists. Administrators of great practical experience have asserted that if the postwar security provisions had obtained during the war, it would not have been possible to have accomplished anything approximating the great successes of wartime scientific research. Some of the consequences of security for science will take years to be uncovered. Only after many years, if ever, will it be known which crucial bits of knowledge lay hidden by classification and had to wait for a long time to be rediscovered by someone else who then made use of them for some important discovery. That such things happen in the history of science is certain even when communication is free. They are even more likely to happen when it is unfree.

It was recently pointed out that if security provisions

such as now exist in the United States had existed in Germany early in the present century the discovery of nuclear energy might not have occurred. Professor Einsten's postulation of the equivalence of mass and energy through the concept of relativity was possible only on the basis of Max Planck's work on high temperature radiation. If present security regulations existed at that time, Einstein might never have known of Planck's work since it would have been classified as relevant to military security.

A scientist, under our present system, might formulate an idea of military importance, but can be excluded from developing it by reason of his not having a "need to know" (in the security sense of the term). Even though he could contribute greatly to its development, compartmentalization within the security system might prevent him from either contributing to, or learning from, subsequent development. Or the idea might be classified at birth, and other scientists who might otherwise have taken it up and been stimulated by it might never learn about it even though they have been "cleared." The idea, however potentially useful, must then wait for a duplicate discovery. We are not referring here to the financial wastefulness of duplicate discoveries such as arise in consequence of our security policies in forcing British work to duplicate American work with no gain to either country. We refer rather to the slowing down of scientific progress, and of the progress of military technology which arises from scientific progress.

Older men, more mature or more resigned, or more satisfied to be indifferent if they are left alone to work as they wish, might not feel as strongly as the younger men to whom science and the pursuit of truth is more than a job and to whom the idea of the scientific community is very precious. Such young scientists, perfectly cleared, might still be pushed away and discouraged from doing the research most needed by the country. They feel restricted and frustrated, and as an eminent scientist with great and continuing responsibility in the administration of scientific research has recently said, "There is a limit to the frustration experienced by the really creative scientist, beyond which his creativeness is destroyed irrespective of his willingness to serve." Thus to the extent that militarily relevant science requires for its prosperity the preservation of the integrity of the scientific community, the damage done to it by the excesses and indiscriminateness of the present loyalty-security system hurts both national defense and the spirit and atmosphere which sustains pure science.

Science is, however, far from being only an instrument to be operated for increasing military power or for contributing to economic well-being. It is one of the highest forms of the expression of man's nature and his freedom. Scientific activity is the activity of free men—not of all free men, but of those who have special gifts and qualifications—and its community is the epitome of the free society. Within itself science provides the model of a free society of reasonable men coordinating themselves voluntarily in the light of a transpersonal standards, their own individual intelligence and the judgment of their qualified peers. No one can be coerced in science into beliefs which are contrary to his convictions, and yet his observance of the transpersonal standards of truth and the judgment of his peers provides the framework which facilitates creativity and yet restrains arbitrariness and mere eccentricity.

The scientific community must not only be free internally—here it is obstructed by compartmentalization and overclassification—but it must also be as free as possible in its external relations. Criteria of admission to the scientific community other than evidence of intellectual quality and the moral standards necessary for scientific work harm that community and prevent it from doing its proper work. It was a demand for loyalty which excluded Professors Szilard, Wigner, von Neumann, Franck, Weisskopf, Meitner and the late Enrico Fermi from the scientific communities in their own countries. The effects of this exclusion and its benefits for science in America are known to all. Yet, in a more certainly conscientious and ostensibly more rational way, the United States government has confined the boundaries of the scientific community, refusing research grants, suspending scientists and denying fellowships on criteria which, although far less brutal, are almost as unrealistic and as irrelevant to truth, national security, or welfare as the Nazi and Fascist criteria.

While, on the one hand, the National Science Foundation, the Atomic Energy Commission, and the U.S. Public Health Service have exerted themselves to attract the best young minds to science and to provide them with the means for prosecuting their research, the security-loyalty policies of the government are unwittingly undoing the government's own work by making the scientific career less attractive and more worrisome and distracting than it must be if creativity in scientific discovery is to be fostered.

The elementary requirements of a sound security program would infringe, to some extent, on the autonomy of science. Some work would have to be classified, and the principle of publicity within the field of science would be somewhat restricted. Some scientists would have to be checked for the reliability in the handling of secret information, and this would introduce a restriction of the autonomy of science in regulating its own membership and its allocation to the various scientific tasks to be undertaken. The intrusions of a realistic security program into the autonomous domain of science would on the whole be marginal and of no great significance to the central concerns of science.

As long, however, as the security program mixes considerations of maximal loyalty with those of security, the area of science over which autonomy obtains is much more restricted, and without gain to science or to the nation. Until the preoccupation with loyalty and particularly with maximal loyalty is eliminated from the field of security, it will continue to be so, despite the quiescence of demagogues and the conscientiousness of security officers. The demagogues, although silent for the time being and perhaps for even longer, may well rest. Their influence is more lasting than the uproar they caused.

CHAPTER 8

POLITICAL DISCOURSE AND

THE SENSE OF AFFINITY

ALTHOUGH POLITICS CREATES STRAIN, and excitement is often its reward, calm and detachment are indispensable for the work of the politician. The politicians who stand at the center of public attention must radiate an air of calm; unless they do the populace becomes disordered or dismayed and the decisions which politicians have to make bear the signs of poor thought, ill-governed impulse and irrelevant emotion. The decisions which politicians and the highest officials of the executive branch have to make are difficult enough, and probably exceed human capacities frequently enough, even when the talents and temperament of the rulers are of the best. They become even more unmanageable when attention is addled and equanimity upset. Passionate speech, aggressive tones, and the metaphors of violence stir parallel and contrary passions in their audience in both elite and populace. Cleavages within the elite are underscored and institutions are either driven apart or united in battle formations. The free and easy mutual confidence, the vague sense of affinity on which the cohesion of civil society, especially at the top, depends, is transformed into brittleness by the language of ideological politics.

The language of political life in the United States has long been thickly veined with excessive vehemence and denunciatory hyperbole. But even in the United States the harshness of political language fluctuates. It has certainly become rougher and more brutal under the impact of the fear of subversion and the worry about the safety of secrets. By a circular process of mutual stimulation a demagogue like Senator McCarthy stirs up the always rankling passions of the nervous Nellies, who imagine Bolsheviks under their beds, the Pope in the White House and the Jews and Communists ruling the world. The crudely aggressive speech which abounds in terms like "rat killing" arouses the dormant anxieties of other persons, who if left alone would not be excessively worried about conspiracy and who would not think of scientific secrets at all. The extremely excitable types probably number no more than a few hundred thousand at most in their pure form, and under ordinary circumstances they are quite harmless to the body politic. Their incapacity for organization and the incapacity of the leaders to whom they give their devotion to organize them and to co-operate with other leaders ordinarily deprive these victims of ideological jitters of weighty political influence through organizations of their own formation.

The situation is different when, within the institutions of civil government, the ideological syndrome appears. When politicians like Senators McCarthy and Jenner, the late Senator McCarran and a dozen lesser but still sputtering lights coalesce and send their united beams flashing through the nation, a section of the population and a strand of sentiment which are ordinarily kept at bay expands. The potential xenophobia, populistic fear of conspiracy, hyperpatriotism and the other elements of the constellation which lies latent in far more people than it dominates, are brought closer to the surface of judgment. The country does not become hysterical — only intellectuals separated by the Atlantic Ocean or by a great spiritual distance are so ignorant of the hold which routine obligations and personal relationships have on the bulk of the population—but uneasiness does move in them. It moves sufficiently for them to assent to the work of the demagogues and for some of them to take their place among the clamant rabble of the ideological fanatics.

The flow of mad letters, which is one of the chief modes of direct influence of the hole-and-corner ideologues on their representatives, increases. This confirms the populistic politician's view that he is speaking with the people's voice.[1] Such crankiness is always going on in the United States, as in Great Britain. But in the United States, rather more frequently than in Great Britain, sections of the political elite do echo this madness in periods of crisis which they then help to aggravate. In Great Britain the alliance of hierarchy, respectability, and the greater capacity of the elite for self-discipline and self-closure, usually confines the lunatics to letter-writing and picketing. Their outcries are muffled by a taciturn elite which is impatient with unseemliness.

The agitation about secrecy and subversion brings into the stream of political life and influence passions and persons who, under better conditions, are covered by obscurity. Frustrated for many years, laboring away in anonymity, they seize the opportunity to emerge into glory in the service of a great cause. The atmosphere is more congenial to their phantasies and hatred. Not only are politicians moved to greater exertion to share in the publicity, but persons who have never received publicity see in the situation a glorious opportunity. The son of an owner of a chain of hotels begins a meteoric career by writing a childish pamphlet on Communism with which his father seeks to rival the Gideon Society by placing a copy in each hotel room under his control. Another young man of less affluent connections is tempted by money and publicity and the ease of destruction to accuse all sorts of persons of being members of the Communist Party. Problematic types with shady pasts turn up at Congressional hearings to claim for themselves the new

---

1. In March, 1953, the House Un-American Activities Committee, searching for a sector of the national elite which other investigators had not yet exploited, thoughtlessly hit upon the clergy. Respectability rallied at once and rebuffed the suggestion. Representative Velde, rattled by a brusque denial of what appeared to him to be a legitimate source of publicity, replied that "people all over the nation have voiced an overwhelming interest in favor of such an investigation and demand the Committee's immediate attention to this particular problem." He said he had received 1,775 letters of which 1,693 were favorable to the investigation of the clergy. Although the texts of the letters have not been made available to the public, previous experience with such letters gives good grounds for believing that they must have been a farrago of madness and ugly hatred.

kind of heroism, the heroism of having been FBI informants within the Communist Party. Failures who could not get on in the careers to which they aspired become investigators of committees inquiring into the subversiveness of philanthropic foundations. A former clergyman, who for years excelled in bad judgment and restless and naive antinomianism, who allowed himself to be led by the nose by Communists and who was then cast out of them because of a disagreement, lends his expertise to investigating bodies in order to have revenge on his faithless friends. Wretched ex-Communists, who for years played with phantasies of destroying American society and harming their fellow citizens, having fallen out with their equally villainous comrades, now provide a steady stream of information and misinformation about the extent to which Communists, as coherent and stable in character as themselves, penetrated and plotted to subvert American institutions. One even tells of how Communists planned to take over that simple and pliant institution, the Army of the United States. Hatred and vengefulness, made free by ignorance and the prospect of reward, produce the information which guides judgment of government officials who were brought up to know better.

Public life becomes the scene of the settlement of private grudges. The Reverend J. B. Matthews, the quondam research director of the House Committee on Un-American Activities and a very transient member of the staff of the Senate Permanent Subcommittee on Investigations, had many grudges to work off against his old friends who had cut him off so coldly and meanly after he had served the cause so faithfully in so many other Communist front organizations. Mr. Paul Crouch, too, has many scores to settle and he is eager to do so as long as the Department of Justice pays him and so are the eighty-odd ex-Communists who continue their careers of personal rancor and hatred.[2] A poor

---

2. This estimate excludes the rightly unknown numbers of spies which the Federal Bureau of Investigation must maintain within Communist Party cells over the country. About these persons nothing can be said. Those who have appeared in public without the approval of the FBI, broken

thing of a refugee without talents and full of spite against his superiors becomes the source of baseless charges against one part of the State Department, a nervous spinster compiles an immense list of names of Communists in the State Department on a roll of wrapping paper for presentation to the Secretary of State. A New York lawyer, dreaming of the Communist seizure of power in his city's schools, offers his cherished works to the educational authorities, while in California another lawyer offers the results of seventeen years of study of Communist influence in school textbooks to show how insidiously the Communists have been at work. Then more obscure, but with a far more massive effect, are the nameless denunciators who supply the derogatory information against government employees and candidates for governmental appointment. They range from responsible and painstakingly careful persons to spiteful neighbors, affronted shopkeepers, angry landlords, resentful janitors, ill-informed students, injured ex-wives and every type of embittered, angry, cranky gossip who feels free to speak in an important role, while feeling safe from the necessity of answering for their protected aggressiveness. Hatred, jealousy, private spites and sheer madness acquire political objects under these conditions and enter into the central arena of the political realm.

Personal ambitions become intricately involved with ideological passions. The poor failures in life who hitherto had only their own ill-fortune, their lack of talent and the personal disfavor of their superiors to blame, now begin to see a possible transfiguration of their misery. Even where there is neither money nor fame available, the gratification of spitefulness is available to former landladies, teachers, classmates, and neighbors whose meager knowledge, suspicious dispositions and vague memories lead them to assert that the person they knew fifteen years ago was a member of

their discipline and appeared before investigating committees of their own initiative, give the same appearance of broken careers, embitterment, shady existences and moral instability. Those who do their unpleasant and scarcely rewarding work in anonymity must be somewhat more solid, although it is a job which, although socially necessary, can hardly be very ennobling.

subversive organizations, read subversive books and papers.

In all parts of American society the preoccupation with secrecy opened up the sluices of lunacy and venom. Within the citizenry and within the government, base passions were allowed to enter into domains from which it was the responsibility of honorable men to exclude them. Commercial enterprises were established, specializing in the assembly of derogatory information about the private lives of prospective employees. They sold their services to employers who feared the ill-repute and financial loss which might arise from the rumor that they employed disloyal persons.

The stream of anxiety formed about the fear of subversion, like the Communist stream of aggressiveness and bitterness against the existing order, swept into itself the many grudges and half-mad angers which it encountered on its path. Checked careers and blighted lives, the down-and-outers and the desperate, found in political enthusiasm, as they often find in religious revivals, a means of re-entering what appeared to them to be a moral life. Moreover, this re-induction into respectability was for some reinforced by the prospect of income and connections which their new convictions offered.

Gradually the tone of speech of the angry and embittered began to color the outlook of the ordinary reasonable man and to make him a little less reasonable. In America, the general etiquette of political discourse is often rude. When the conventional roughness and overstatement was fused with the imagery of the political paranoiac, the result was a steadily deteriorating situation. A competition of anti-subversion developed. Persons who were previously unconcerned began to vie with one another in anti-Communism. Speech became more intemperate in the race to catch attention, to keep one's job or to hold one's constituency.

The respectable part of society was, of course, put at an enormous disadvantage in its relations with such demagogy. The conflict which is always stirring between these two elements was in part hampered by the respectable element's effort to render the demagogues powerless by beating them at their own game of demagogy. This made it more difficult for them to rally to use the only techniques which were really available to them: constitutional procedures, political combination, and the assertion of the rightfulness and dignity of the respectable position. The disadvantage of respectability was aggravated by its half-hearted alliance with demagogy, which it regarded as a possibly useful if not wholly likeable ally. The difficulties of President Eisenhower and his supporters with the demagogues arose from this uncertainty about the effectiveness of the procedures which have for the time being once more proved effective, and from their thoughtlessness about the dangers of the alliance.

The nearly ten-year-long disturbance of public peace by the angry quest for publicity about conspiracy and by baseless worries about secrecy has left wounds on American society from which it cannot soon recover. The decade's events hurt the delicate tissue which binds our society together. Even if we disregard the pariahs whose failure to obtain clearance has resulted in a partial loss of civil rights, the memory of this mean-spirited and ungenerous decade will linger for a long time. The Democratic Party will not forget for a few years yet the canard of "twenty years of treason," and that will coarsen the already rough texture of American political life. Nor will all the persons called forth, with passions aroused, from the sinks and corners of society crawl back into the dull obscurity in which they lived before. Proximity to the stage will be too tempting for some of them, and they will hang about looking for a political brawl in which they can once more feel the excitement of ideological battle.

Moreover, once institutional practices last a decade and establish a specialized personnel with vested interests in their jobs and procedures, they are extremely hard to eradicate. The security profession will in a way see to it that the present atmosphere of mutual distrust is maintained, not by deliberate malice, but just because that is the way many of them see the world and its problems.

Thus even if the memory of this period of uncivil politics could be forgotten, the vested interests in its continuance would carry it along. The memories are not, however, to be uprooted so easily. They fit too well into the fundamental distrust towards politics which runs diffusely throughout American life and which is strongest in the educated classes. The American intelligentsia would have had enough obstacles in the way of overcoming a tradition of more than a century, and their ill-ordered political education of the 1930's and their four years of realistic patriotism during the Second World War would probably not have sufficed to clear their minds of prejudice and to set them on the right path of civil politics. Still, the twelve years from 1933 to 1945, although they covered many silly detours, moved in the right direction. The decade since the war was a reversal of their education. It confirmed, by the volubility and zeal of a minority of congressmen, journalists, radio commentators, etc., their old prejudices against politics and politicians. The apparent disappearance of radical political alienation among college and university students should not be overestimated. The aesthetic and religious interests of the more sensitive are themselves forms of antipolitical reaction. Under the surface, fear and hatred of a vague bogey called McCarthyism, which is not too divergent in their minds from the pattern of ordinary politics, is boiling. Having undergone the long corruption of Communist infiltration, youthful radicalism—an inevitable and often admirable occurrence in our society—has now had its vision further beclouded by extremist anti-Communism. It has become cramped and intimidated and has been encouraged in its incorrect view of the world.

There is no danger of this suppressed youthful radicalism becoming revolutionary—even less than the fellow-travelling movements of the 1930's could or would have brought about a revolution. The danger of revolution is not a problem in the United States and was not in the 1930's, 1940's, or 1950's. The more serious problem is the disjunction of the spheres and in particular the cleavages among politicians and intellectuals. The nurture of a better sense of affinity between the two groups is one of the main problems of American public life, and to its solution the past ten years have contributed only additional difficulties.

CHAPTER 9

THE PRIVATE SPHERE

SECRECY IS PRIVACY made compulsory. With more severe sanctions for the disclosure of information, more emphatic demands for its withholding from persons authorized to receive it, secrecy appears to be an extension of privacy. It is privacy with higher, more impassable barriers. Yet secrecy is the enemy of privacy.

In order for secrets to be safeguarded, privacy must be invaded. The security of secrets has come to require not only physical security and classification; it requires very understandably the selection of personnel. The science of personnel selection for the reliable handling of secret information is still unborn. The administrators of security are, however, sufficiently "psychological" in their outlook to understand that the observance or the breach of security is neither accidental nor simply a function of bribery. The idea that the breaches in security are dependent on dispositional factors—such as political attitudes or personal propensities —is the foundation of the disruption of privacy by secrecy. The protection of security, even when it is undistorted by the demand for loyalty *qua* loyalty, compels those responsible for it to enquire extensively into the attitudes of the person to be entrusted with secret information.

The object of the quest is any quality of the person which would lead him to disregard the barrier of secrecy. It might be political conviction; it might be compulsive disloyalty; it might be some quality of character which is only indirectly related to secrecy, but which might cause the person in question to come into a situation in which he could be coerced into disclosure of his secret knowledge.

Unlike the traditional pluralistic standards of professional selection which focused on technical qualifications for the efficient performance of the task and which involved only an examination of educational qualifications, prior professional experience, and estimates of the extent to which qualities of character would permit satisfactory collaboration with colleagues—none of which called for information outside these categories—the system of personnel selection borne of security must go far beyond those narrow limits. It requires extensive investigation of sources of information of which the individual investigated is unaware, or at least does not bring forward. His own testimonials are suspect and information must be sought from other sources.

Since it is not likely in most cases that he has broken security regulations in the past, the enquiry must deal only lightly with the extent to which he has actually observed security regulations or broken them. The investigation aims rather to discover facts which are thought, on the basis of quite unverified assumptions, to indicate a probability of breaking security. Since there is no adequate scientific indicator of the probability of infringement on security regulations, the quest is unbounded. Every aspect of the person's life is enquired into in the search for the indeterminate clues as to whether he might in the future do something he has never done before.

The net must be cast widely because the investigator has no precise expectation regarding the predispositions of unreliability in the observance of security rules. Almost any quality is relevant and even the most narrowly delimited criterion such as political affiliations soon leads off into many highly ramified by-ways of personal friendship, relationship by marriage or blood, casual acquaintanceships, etc.

The assessment of the potential unreliability of the investigated person rests on "derogatory information." It is not our point here that the search for derogatory information encourages malice, spitefulness, and denunciation. The significant point is that the derogatory information is not confined to categories of activity which give fully valid indications of prospective infringement of security rules. Political affiliation or association or sympathy is not a very good clue.

Only a negligible proportion of the Communists who have been dismissed from the government or who have been investigated prior to or after their resignations are alleged to have been spies at any time, to say nothing of having been such during a period of more stringent security regulations. Hence being a Communist or having been one, although it enhances the likelihood of breaches of security, is not a very good indicator. It becomes necessary, therefore, to go into the person's private life, beyond his political activity and outlook.

It is pertinent here to cite the list of criteria for security clearance in Category B¹ of the Atomic Energy Commission. Although one of the most "sensitive" government bodies, its security system is also the most scrupulously administered. A strict effort, unfortunately not always successful, is made to exclude irrelevancies and to avoid the temptations of hyperpatriotism.

"Category B includes those cases in which there are grounds sufficient to establish a reasonable belief that with respect to the individual or his spouse there is:

"1. Sympathetic interest in totalitarian, Fascist, Communist, or other subversive political ideologies;

"2. A sympathetic association established with members of the Communist Party; or with leading members of any organization which has been declared to be subversive by the Attorney General. (Ordinarily this would not include chance or casual meetings, nor contacts limited to normal business or official relations.)

"3. Identification with an organization established as a front for otherwise subversive groups or interests when the personal views of the individual are sympathetic to or coincide with subversive 'lines';

"4. Identification with an organization known to be in-

---

1. Category A is more narrowly concentrated on the facts of unreliability, e.g., attempts to commit or to aid others to commit acts of "sabotage, espionage, treason, or sedition"; "association with espionage agents of a foreign nation"; past violations of security regulations "to a degree which would endanger the common defense or national security," etc.

filtrated with members of subversive groups when there is also information as to other activities of the individual which establishes the probability that he may be a part of or sympathetic to the infiltrating element, or when he has personal views which are sympathetic to or coincide with subversive 'lines';

"5. Residence of the individual's spouse, parent(s), brother(s), sister(s), or offspring in a nation whose interests may be inimical to the interests of the United States, or in satellites or occupied areas thereof, when the personal views or activities of the individual subject of investigation are sympathetic to or coincide with subversive 'lines' (to be evaluated in the light of the risk that pressure applied through such close relatives could force the individual to reveal sensitive information or perform an act of sabotage);

"6. Close continuing association with individuals (friends, relatives or other associates) who have subversive interests and associations as defined in any of the foregoing types of derogatory information. A close continuing association may be deemed to exist if:

(1) Subject lives at the same premises with such individual;

(2) Subject visits such individual frequently;

(3) Subject communicates frequently with such individual by any means.

"7. Association where the individuals have enjoyed a very close, continuing association such as is described above for some period of time, and then have been separated by distance; provided the circumstances indicate that a renewal of contact is probable;

"Category B also includes those cases in which there are grounds sufficient to establish a reasonable belief that with respect to the individual there is:

"8. Conscientious objection to service in the Armed Forces during time of war, when such objections cannot be clearly shown to be due to religious convictions;

"9. Manifest tendencies demonstrating unreliability or inability to keep important matters confidential; wilful or

gross carelessness in revealing or disclosing to any unauthorized person restricted data or other classified matter pertain-
ing either to projects of the Atomic Energy Commission or
of any other governmental agency; abuse of trust, dishonesty,
or homosexuality."

Paragraphs 5, 6, 7 and 9 carry the inquiry into the very
center of what has always been regarded under individualist liberalism as "none of anybody's business." In the case
of the Atomic Energy Commission the information gathered
in these forays into the once private sphere are strictly
guarded. In the case of Dr. Oppenheimer, however, the effort to keep the private secret was suspended and information which, if it had to be gathered, need never have been
disclosed, was released to the public. Details of Dr. Oppenheimer's personal, once private life, were published in the
record of the testimony which could have been omitted, if
not from the hearings, then certainly from the printed text.
The sections of the proceedings in which the contents of
classified documents were adduced were "off the record."
Could not privacy have been respected equally with secrecy?

Even a body as self-confining in its concern with functional secrecy as the Atomic Energy Commission shows the
influence of the populistic mentality in such a situation.
What restriction of the public's capacity for independent
judgment would have been created by the omission of certain details of Dr. Oppenheimer's personal relations? If
classified data require a legitimate restriction of what is exposed to the public, could not respect for privacy have permitted an equally legitimate restriction?

The intrusion into the individual's private sphere and
the tinge of fundamental disrespect for it is more substantial
in the security-loyalty policies of other agencies. In all this
disruption of individual privacy there is a peculiar concomi-
tant which is strange to an individualistic liberal tradition.
This is the anti-individualistic assumption that an individual
is not morally independent and that he shares an "essence"
with his kin. If his kin are Communists or Communist sympathizers, then the individual, too, must participate in the

"spirit" which dominates them. There is a further anti-individualist assumption in the doctrine of guilt by association or kinship. That is the idea that if two persons are in contact, it must always be the wicked one who triumphs over the good. It would never be regarded as an argument on behalf of a Communist sympathizer's security reliability that he has non-Communist friends; it is almost always counted against a non-Communist that he has friends who are Communists or Communist sympathizers. The conclusion is clear: the non-Communist is always susceptible to the superior power of his Communist associate. Again, the strength of individuality, the basis of privacy, is denied in the search for secrecy.

If such transformations of the pluralistic individualistic outlook occur where conscientious and matter-of-fact officials seek to find the best technical means of selecting reliable employees for work on secret matters, the situation is naturally more extreme among those for whom secrecy is of symbolic value. Congressional investigating committees have never been respecters of privacy. Their populistic origin and atmosphere render that almost inconceivable.

One of the most egregious instances of the decay of the sense of privacy in governmental and journalistic circles occurred when the uproar about subversion and secrecy was at its highest. In the spring of 1953 an employee of the Voice of America, worried about the prospect of an attack by a Congressional investigating committee, committed suicide. He was not under investigation at that time, had not been investigated previously, and even the incidents following his death did not reveal anything bearing on security. He had written a long letter to his wife explaining his side of the case, which revolved around the location of two long-range transmitters. It was found in a sealed envelope on his body. The policeman turned the letter over to the county medical examiner. The latter official, for no reason other than being possessed by the belief that any action of a government official involved subversion in some way, gave the letter to the Federal Bureau of Investigation, which sent copies of the letter to Washington. The county medical examiner then telephoned the State Department and read the letter to an official there. The State Department, well trained to anticipate the demands of Congressional investigators, gave a copy of the letter to Senator McCarran who announced that he would investigate "certain aspects" of the letter. From Congress, the letter was released to the press. Then finally the Associated Press, at the request of the family, sent the widow the text of the letter which had been addressed to her and which she had never seen.

This unjustifiable transgression of the right of privacy with its immediate invocation of the Federal Bureau of Investigation occurred in one of the centers most devoted to Senator McCarthy and his war against the subversive and the educated.

The distrust of privacy is the distrust of the individual's capacity for judgment and self-government. It is a phenomenon of religious revivalism, which asserts that man's highest moments are those when he is permeated by the "spirit." In this case the spirit is the national spirit and a person who withholds himself in a sphere of privacy is denying the legitimacy of the national "spirit." The infusion of the mind with hyperpatriotism is thought by the zealots of secrecy and publicity to be the only means of overcoming the evil which must otherwise dominate the personality. Privacy is waywardness, from the point of view of "enthusiasm," and waywardness is wickedness.[2]

---

2. This interpretation of the hatred of privacy as in part a product of a secular false religion of hyperpatriotism and maximal loyalty finds some support in Senator McCarthy's repeated use of the term "purge." He frequently has invited present and former Communists and fellow-travellers to come forward in the hearings of his committee and "purge" themselves of their moral contamination. From this point of view, subversion and conspiracy are not actions, but states of mind. (Senator McCarthy at the height of his power seldom concerned himself with actions; almost always with attitudes and associations.) The wrongful state of mind can be overcome only by hyperpatriotism. Under the conditions created by such beliefs it is easy to see that privacy would be dealt with rather roughly.

CHAPTER 10

THE PROTECTION OF SECURITY

I. Secrecy and Pluralism

THE MAINTENANCE of a functionally necessary secrecy can never be a completely harmonious part of the system of publicity and privacy, essential to the free society. Secrecy is foreign to the pluralistic institutional system, in which there are no impermeable walls between institutions and in which withholding and disclosure are voluntary.

A pluralistic society, while not a totally "open" society is nonetheless largely so. It offers opportunity of movement from occupation to occupation, depending on capacity. It permits free communication within spheres and between them to the extent that there is the desire for such communication. It grants freedom of personal association across the boundaries of institutions; it forbids prescription or proscription in the selection of associates.

Secrecy as part of a security system is an imperative imposed by the need of the society to preserve itself and the values which it embodies, and even though it is alien to the pluralistic society, it is necessary for it as well. Security discriminates in the regulation of access to certain key positions in the society and prevents the entry by persons who might use the knowledge gained in these positions for the benefit of an enemy or potential enemy. The discrimination is necessarily based on the scrutiny of an individual's past and the formation of estimates of his future conduct. As such, it is an intrusion in the private sphere. Security limits the freedom of communication from these key positions. In several very important respects, therefore, even functionally necessary security brings with it encroachments on the freedom of selection of personnel and the principles of publicity and privacy which pluralism grants to spheres of activity, to individuals and to corporate bodies. Freedom permits and encourages alienation from authority. Injustice and the irrational hatred of society create inner enemies whose organized action must be the object of safeguards.

Conspirators and revolutionaries have existed in all countries, in the most repressive and the most just, and they cannot be entirely eliminated. It should be remembered, however, that none of the great bourgeois societies with a long tradition of freedom and a substantial middle class has experienced a Communist revolution. Great Britain is perfectly secure from revolution; France, which was the classic country of pre-Marxian revolution and which has the sharpest cleavages in its social structure, has been secure too. The Scandinavian and the Low Countries likewise seem to be reasonably safe. The United States, which has never even had an influential Socialist movement, would appear to a detached observer to be the last country in the world in which a Communist revolution could take place. Nonetheless, one may grant that, given the nature of Bolshevism, a certain amount of precautionary action is in order in the United States as well as in other liberal countries.

Even if there were no trace of revolutionary sentiment whatsoever within the United States, certain security measures would still be necessary to prevent espionage on behalf of potential enemies. When potentially enemy states are joined with the minor bits and pieces of the domestic revolutionary movement, then security measures are certainly urgent. Their urgency arises not from the probability of Communist revolution in the United States—that must be estimated as entirely improbable—but because the Communist movement in the United States has aided the espionage activities of the Soviet Union.

II. *The Control of Subversion and Espionage*

The task of a security agency is to see that revolutionaries and spies do no damage by getting into positions in which their espionage, sabotage or subversion can make a significant difference to the stability of the social order. The task has become more complicated since revolutionary movements have become able to practice the technique of infiltration into the government. To the task of physical security, the management of personnel security has been added. The selection of personnel to occupy positions in which they will deal with secret information entails prior knowledge of the personnel of revolutionary organizations as well as a capacity to assess moral qualities. The former kind of knowledge is acquired through the scrutiny of publications, through the testimony of former members and through the reports of security agents within the revolutionary or espionage organizations. The tracing of memberships in revolutionary parties is more difficult when the party is compartmentalized into small units as a defensive measure. The greater the external pressure the more insulated become its links with espionage and correspondingly the more difficult to trace from within the party. Increased compartmentalization restricts the range of knowledge available to any undercover agent and multiplies many times the number required. Reliable undercover agents are hard to find since the task is rewarding neither psychologically nor financially.

When the party goes underground its publications become less revealing and scarcer and the organization as a whole is more difficult to perceive. Moreover, when a party is illegal its watchfulness over new members is greater and entry is more difficult to accomplish.

Can laws which declare the Communist Party illegal, which require registration of its members and which declare illegal membership in the party when it is accompanied by awareness of the Party's revolutionary aims, contribute much to the internal security of the nation? It will certainly weaken the Communist Party as an organization capable of influencing opinion and of revolutionary action, but the Party was never strong enough to be a basis for realistic concern. If the party persists as an illegal organization these laws will not facilitate its surveillance by the FBI. It will obstruct the tracing of the network through which spies might transmit material or be recruited. If the Communist Party ceases to exist as a recruiting ground for spies, then the links into spy rings will be lost and the discovery of espionage networks will remain as accidental a process as it has always been. The hindrance of the Communist Party's provision of a large reservoir of persons from whom a small number of spies might be recruited is on the other hand a gain for security—although it should be remembered that espionage and treason are not dependent solely on ideological loyalty. On balance, perhaps, the laws which attack the Party and its membership do make Soviet espionage a little more difficult while it also makes counterintelligence more difficult at the same time.

The law which would withdraw the citizenship of members of the Communist Party contributes nothing to security. To initiate such action against a Communist assumes that it is already known that he is a Communist, in which case there are more than ample security provisions to keep him out of "sensitive" positions within the government or in private industry. It adds practically nothing to the incentives to shun Communism. It proposes no new technique for discerning the activities which are dangerous to social order. It only adds another penalty to the other penalties already available for the same crime.

Such a law might well be successful with some persons, the more timorous and the more respectable, who would in any case probably not be inclined towards subversion. The desperate person, already embittered and hateful towards the existing society and feeling himself an outsider would be less affected by the prospective loss of his citizenship. Such persons do not prize their citizenship highly and might even despise it. Often many foreign-born Communists have been in the United States for years without becoming naturalized. The hard-bitten, deeply alienated person will not be deterred.

What about the cynical enemy of the civil order, well-educated, sophisticated, and respectable in appearance? He will be deterred only insofar as the loss of citizenship obstructs his revolutionary aims. For example, it might deter a person who serves the revolutionary cause as a lawyer from joining the Party, when the loss of his citizenship would render the pursuit of his profession impossible; or if he must be a citizen in order to have public employment, which is necessary for his work of subversion and espionage, he will not enter the Party but will serve it without actual formal affiliation.

The chief victims of such a law will be the simple-minded and the naive, the romantic young people who join revolutionary movements because of their ignorant generosity of spirit and their adolescent love of the atmosphere of secrecy and danger. They are not likely to remain revolutionaries as they mature and assume adult responsibilities. They cease, from uninterestedness, boredom, and repulsion for the cold and inhuman character of the "hard core" of Communist fanatics. They are the most likely victims of the deprivation of citizenship and they are the persons who should be the most protected from it. The law which would deprive them of their citizenship would isolate them and prevent their assimilation into civil society. It would alienate them from their society at a time when they are most ready to be assimilated into it. Instead of becoming citizens in the deeper sense of the word, the withdrawal of their citizenship would confirm, for some of them, the revolutionary views which they would otherwise renounce. The maintenance of a pluralistic society in which there are few "outsiders" would be obstructed by a law which would create a class of unassimilable pariahs.

The law which has recently been enacted to punish peacetime espionage by death might be more effective in the maintenance of secrecy. Yet if this law reflects a desire for the cruel punishment of spies rather than the conduct of effective counterespionage, it might not be so helpful. The most important element in counterespionage activities is to trace out the network, penetrate the organization and frustrate it as its most crucial point. The frustration of espionage activity, based on meticulous, long and elaborate investigation is more important than the punishment of spies who if prematurely exposed and punished bring to an end the possibility of tracing their ramifications and neutralizing them.

There is another objection to this law. It furthers the brutalization of the standards of public judgment which are already harsh enough during crisis periods. The delicate texture of the sense of affinity which constitutes the matrix of the autonomy of groups and individuals is torn by crude aggressiveness of tone and deed. The decision to add the death penalty was the product of a situation in which the principles of civility were already weakened in some part and it contributes towards the persistence of that weakened state. The addition of the death penalty in peacetime for a crime for which severe penalties already exist, lowers the threshold of the permissible in civil life.[1]

The policy of personnel security which obtains under Executive Order 10450, the Atomic Energy Act, and the Summary Dismissal Act, is probably as effective as any security program can be, reckoning with the universal limitations in capacity for the assessment of human propensities and the nondescript qualifications of some security officers. There is no evidence at hand to show that any spies or links with spies have survived the scrutiny of the system. The system can never attain perfection, and the less the Soviet Union depends on American Communists and Communist sympathizers to help them organize their espionage in this country, the further it will be removed from perfection. The present system is centered around the assumption that spies are recruited from among those who feel an ideological kinship with the Soviet Union and from those who can be

---

1. It is not a far cry from this law to Governor Shivers' recent recommendation that the death penalty should be inflicted on Communists. It is evidence of the competition of aggressiveness and of the deterioration of standards. That Governor Shivers' proposal was not taken up is a tribute to the strength of civil morality in America. That the death penalty for peacetime espionage was enacted into law is evidence that its strength is not unqualified.

blackmailed or personally influenced or who by loose and careless talk disclose the secrets which have been entrusted to them. This seems a narrow and doctrinaire conception of the motives of treasonable conduct. It is this narrow doctrinairism which makes the present personnel security system so inefficient, even though it might well be fairly effective. Although it might catch a few potential spies, it hurts many innocent persons. The resources marshalled against the potential spy are usually almost equally dangerous to the innocent; the conception of potentiality is so wide and so vague that many of the innocent are treated as if they were likely to become spies. Injustice is done and much rancor has been generated throughout the educated classes. For reasons which we shall set forth at the end of this chapter, it is doubtful if fishing for spies with such a fine net and at such political and moral cost is worth while.

The Administration does not have the responsibility for the creation of the present *security* program. Much of the impetus for it has come from the legislative body. It is not very feasible to separate out the contributions of the two branches to the program, particularly since much of the pressure for the program has come from the legislative body. Nonetheless, the component of *loyalty* in the present Administration's program is owed largely to the legislative branch. The latent demand for maximal loyalty which surrounds the whole program is the creature of the legislature, although the administration, and the Truman even more than the Eisenhower administration, must bear a fair share of the blame.

III. Maximum Loyalty and Security

The spearhead of the war for maximal loyalty has been the Congressional investigating committees. It is almost their creation. What has the demand for maximal loyalty and the work of the investigating committees contributed to American internal security?

Specifically, even within their own conception of themselves, they have probably achieved very little. The conviction of Alger Hiss for perjury, the indictment of Owen Lattimore for perjury, the indictment of Val Lorwin for perjury, the conviction of William Remington for perjury, the repeated investigation and ultimate dismissal of John P. Davies, the dismissal of John Carter Vincent, and a multitude of dismissals of lesser persons in the government, in universities, and in private industry for claiming the protection of the 5th Amendment—these are perhaps the greatest direct victories of the investigating committees in campaigns.

Alger Hiss at the time of his conviction had been out of government employment for several years. It has not been claimed that he was still active as a member of a Soviet spy ring. The actions which aroused the desire to persecute him for perjury had occurred more than a decade earlier. There is no reason to believe that the documents transferred by Alger Hiss had weakened the United States. The conviction of Alger Hiss was not a reinforcement of American security, although it was a genuine success for the House-Un-American Activities Committee.

The charges against Owen Lattimore were charges of perjury, and the crimes of which he is implicitly accused include neither espionage nor subversion. The substantive acts, if such they can be called, of which Mr. Lattimore was implicitly accused were not crimes at the time they were committed. In any case, his connection with the Department of State had ceased by the time the Senate Subcommittee on Internal Security had begun to pay attention to him. The espionage and sabotage which he might have committed had come to an end and he was in no position to take them up again.

William Remington was convicted of perjury in having denied his membership in the Communist Party—in itself at that time not illegal. He was not charged explicitly with espionage or sabotage, although Miss Bentley did include him in the list of spies with whom she had trafficked in her days as a courier.

Mr. Val Lorwin was mendaciously charged with perjury in connection with events which were alleged to have occurred nearly two decades before; they were not crimes when they were said to have occurred, and the government showed how little confidence it had in its own arguments when it dropped the case under ignominious circumstances.

Mr. John P. Davies was repeatedly cleared of the charges against him. When he was finally dismissed it was because of "poor judgment," a failing having nothing to do with espionage.

The committees have been occupied with every aspect of the complex of problems which center around security and loyalty. They have not aided in the clarification of the distinction. Indeed they have worked in the opposite direction by the vagueness of their charges and the breadth of their pronouncements.

By their stress on complete or maximal loyalty, they have increased the pressure against privacy; and the use, in personnel selection, of crude standards of loyalty as indicators of prospective unreliability in security is the fruit of the long years of work begun by Martin Dies and his colleagues. The insistence that a man's entire life be exposed to the public as a guarantee of his virtue and the belief that every action or sentiment a man has ever experienced is of direct relevance in the constitution of his public loyalty must be counted among the results of the committees' exertions. The technique of the AEC in the case of Dr. Oppenheimer owes much indirectly to the committees.

The greatest positive achievement has been the pressure which led to the loyalty-security program within the executive branch and its unsteady progress since 1947. It is quite possible that this program would have been established at about the same time and in the same manner by the Truman Administration, simply on the basis of the increasing sensitivity to espionage attendant on the deterioration of Soviet-American relations, the Nunn May and Fuchs cases and the Canadian Royal Commission Report as well as the discoveries of the FBI and the Grand Jury. However, it is certainly likely that the House Un-American Activities Committee by its persistent attack on Communists and fellow-travellers in the government pushed the government into the direction which it actually took. It made the administration feel the political necessity of displaying some concern with the dangers of subversion and espionage. But Congressional influence stressed the loyalty rather than the security aspect, the attitude rather than the performance.

IV. *Loyalty*

Even since then the security program has been a sailboat at the mercy of powerful winds. When the committees were at their most passionate, the functionaries of the program were wildly blown about. Security officers became more strict and suspicious, boards more negative and cases once cleared were reopened and reviewed. Even the powerful United States Army did not feel that it was in a position to resist the force of Senator McCarthy and his committee, once McCarthy discovered Dr. Peress boring from within the dental clinic. The Army determined that security risks were to be immediately discharged "under other than an honorable condition."[2]

Loyalty oaths, in which state governments specialized, and with which the Federal Government has had considerable experience, are primarily ceremonial. This is not to say that loyalty oaths are inconsequential. They are useful as a basis for the legal dismissal or the prosecution of employees who are the members of a proscribed organization. Furthermore, the threat of dismissal, rendered real by the actuality of dismissals attended by publicity, does undoubtedly deter some persons from becoming members of such organizations.

Nevertheless, one may say that the loyalty oath is of

---

2. Some of Senator McCarthy's admirers, even those whose admiration was qualified, said that he at least forced the administration to be more scrupulous in its procedures. Nothing could be less true. Random aggressiveness and excessive distrust are no better than laxity.

more significance to those who impose it than it is in the reinforcement of the internal security system of the country. Like vindictive and cruel punishments, loyalty oaths gratify the need for the reaffirmation of moral values which many kinds of persons—in all societies—require in times of crisis. Its real significance is in the confidence in his own values which it brings to the person who punishes and who forces an oath on another person. The argument that loyalty oaths actually create loyalty in those who take the oath is an afterthought.

This is not at all to say that the taking of an oath is completely without significance to the person who takes it. It has the same function of reaffirming values and moral standards already held by the person. A person who is already loyal might be strengthened somewhat in his loyalty —especially if he does not feel that those who are requiring the oath are themselves unworthy of the values to which the oath attests. When false priests administer it, an enforced oath is actually likely to have an alienating effect, though perhaps not a very profound one.

If, however, the oaths are intended to prevent subversion, espionage, and sabotage, they are doomed to failure. An oath which stresses the sacredness of the values inherent in the existing order cannot move those for whom the existing order is the realm of evil. For them the oath is a mockery and its only binding force is the danger of dismissal or fine and arrest for betraying the oath. If, however, the penalties attached to the oath are less severe than those imposed for espionage and sabotage, the spy or saboteur who is willing to take the chance of punishment in order to steal and transmit documents or to damage crucial mechanisms is not likely to be deterred by the lesser punishments which would come to him for breaking his oath. Spies and saboteurs are deeply and aggressively alienated against their own societies. They must be so in order to be able to bring themselves to the performance of actions which they clearly know or dimly feel will hurt their own country. Such people are as unlikely to be deterred by oaths as rubber bands stretched around a building would be to protect it from the destructive power of an atomic bomb.

V. *The Benefit of Secrecy*

Oaths of allegiance are part of the ceremonial of solidarity. They carry no weight in the protection of the security of a country because that must be concerned with the gravely alienated. Loyalty oaths are part of the process of drawing the line around the society of the loyal and excluding the disloyal from participation in that society.[3]

Even when the products of espionage are considerable, it is still far from certain that espionage is either very harmful to its victims or very beneficial to its instigators. The knowledge that one is penetrating to the secrets of the other side is reassuring and strengthening to the morale of the power which gains the secrets. It is more doubtful whether the knowledge gained by espionage makes so much difference. There are so many famous instances of secrets successfully penetrated by spies and then disregarded by those charged with action on the basis of the knowledge so obtained.[4]

In order for the knowledge obtained by espionage to be used, it must pass through a very elaborate process of analysis and through many offices. The probability of being mislaid or passed over in the heavy flow of material is certainly not negligible. Then when it reaches the person who can utilize it he is faced with the question as to whether it can be trusted. Spies are not esteemed by their superiors

---

3. They are one element in the process ostracising the imperfectly loyal from occupations and associations, depriving them of the permission to leave the country if they are not deportable, and deporting them if that can be done. The reason for deporting one alleged Communist (Ignatz Mezei) was given by an Assistant United States Attorney: Mezei was "a Communist all his adult life and doomed to sin in perpetuity because he doesn't know how to do otherwise." The imagery is significant.

4. The Soviet Union, for example, through its network of spies obtained quite exact information regarding the military intentions of the Germans in 1941. There is no evidence that they took action to forestall or frustrate the German plans which they had. There are many other similar cases.

and they are often the victims of "plants" of false information. On many occasions the uncertainty as to whether the data reported by a spy are true, false or planted, results in inaction. Finally, intelligence staffs, even if they arrive at firm conclusions, must contend with the operational side, and just as spies are not esteemed by their masters, the intelligence is not always esteemed by politicians and the military men who are outside the intelligence services. The chances of utilization of the information diminishes at every stage.

Furthermore, many of the objects of espionage are symbolic or conventional rather than realistic. Espionage regarding a nation's foreign policy seems futile when its policy is in operation for all to see. It is also futile because policies are not formulated as recipes, but are the pattern underlying many specific actions—a pattern which except in its most general principles is often not formulated by those who follow it, and which, in those general outlines, is visible to those against whom it is practiced.

Espionage concerning the location of factories, laboratories and military installations might well be desirable for the United States in coping with the Soviet Union, but it is scarcely necessary for the Soviet Union in its action towards the United States. From telephone directories, public and governmental, from newspaper articles, from technical periodicals, practically all significant sites in the United States can be located. The United States is still too devoted to the principles of publicity and privacy, and of the pluralistic society of which they are a part, to suppress all these sources of information in order to keep them from the intelligence service of potential enemies.

Espionage regarding scientific matters, from which the present hullabaloo has obtained much of its vehemence, is also greatly overrated. It can make some difference, but not a very great deal. If a nation like Russia has scientists and a scientific tradition, the secrets with which it must contend are the secrets of nature, not the secrets of the United States. The technical and scientific secrets of the United

States would be good to have, but the fundamental principles of science are available far beyond the borders of the United States and, from those, the content of America's secrets can be obtained without the benefit of espionage.

There remain, of course, many specific matters which must be kept secrets, e.g., cryptographic and cryptoanalytic knowledge. The size of stockpiles might well be kept secret although there are definitely situations in which accurate knowledge by the enemy of one's own resources might be a powerful deterrent to the enemy from any aggressive action. Tactical plans in diplomacy and military operations must be kept secret. All of these, however, constitute a far smaller area of the secret than is demanded by the psychological fascination of secrecy and the passions of maximal loyalty.

The questions then remain: Has the tremendous disturbance and degradation which America has suffered from its own zealots of secrecy and loyalty been worth while? Has the increment to our national security been great enough to justify all the distraction and injustice? Are the secrets we have sought to guard so essential to our national life that it has been worthwhile raising so much passion, injuring so many persons and harming so many institutions? Undoubtedly, the answer is: No.

PART IV

Pluralism Against Extremism

CHAPTER 11

PLURALISTIC POLITICS

PLURALISM IS NOT a single political position. It is the postulate of numerous political positions. Conservatism and liberalism, laissez-faire and socialism, traditionalism and rationalism, hierarchy and equalitarianism, can all fall within the area of pluralism. Pluralism is conservative by contrast with revolutionary extremism, pluralism is liberal by contrast with reactionary extremism. It is only by contrast with the extremes of alienation from social order and orderly change that pluralism appears to be a single position.

Conflict and diversity, change and criticism, are integral to the mutuality of pluralism. So is the order based on affinity. No single party can ever claim that its position and its position alone embodies pluralistic principles. A moderate socialist party, a moderate bourgeois party, a moderate party of small businessmen, a moderate party of big businessmen, a moderate Christian party, a moderate freethinker's party, a regional party, and above the parties which amalgamate many traditions and interests like the American parties can all fall within the circle of pluralism. What places them there is the moderation of their demands, their desire for a little more of what they think is good rather than the complete and immediate fulfillment of every dream and impulse.

Parties and beliefs which are satisfied to remain within the circle of pluralism define their goals, regardless of their substantive content, as small increments. A socialist party, whose socialist aspirations are fulfilled when, as in Great Britain, publicly operated institutions, industries, and services, employ 25% of the gainfully occupied as compared with 15% before the introduction of socialism, and a conservative party which accepts the principle of health insurance but

225

thinks that it should be done through private initiative and through privately owned insurance institutions, which, in other words, is satisfied if the standard of private responsibility is respected, can both equally be pluralistic in the social policy and politics which they espouse.

Pluralistic politics is marked also by the moderation of political involvement. A lukewarm "politicization" is a feature of pluralistic politics. This is particularly so among the lower levels of the membership of the political bodies, but it must obtain, at least relatively, among the elites. Politicians in a pluralistic society must be more than politicians, even though politics engages most of their energy and interest. They must also be concerned with objects other than political objects and they must look at them from a nonpolitical point of view. Politicians must enjoy the excitement of the political conflict or they would not care to be politicians; but if most of them care only for that the boundaries of pluralism will be overrun.

Pluralistic politics, regardless of political standpoint or platform, requires from its practitioners a spread of interest beyond the range of politics; it also prohibits emotional intensity, especially emotional excitement continuing over long stretches of time or running on without intermission. Intense passions at election time do not harm pluralism if they fade away quickly thereafter and do not flare up except momentarily between elections.

The apocalyptic mentality sees every issue as a conflict between diametrically opposed alternatives, and it sees the carriers of these alternatives as opposed to each other completely, fundamentally and continuously. The pluralistic mentality, believing the alternatives fall within a narrower range, believes also that the proponents of the alternatives also have more in common with each other than do apocalyptic politicians. The smaller the gap between the alternatives, the closer the positions of their proponents, so that the fundamental political positions are separated from each other, not by deep cleavages or disjunctions, but by gradual variations. Thus, small increments of achievement are acceptable because all pluralist politics rejects the apocalyptic point of view which counts as important only the differences between salvation and damnation. While small increments of achievement are valued, small variations in the properties of associates, colleagues, and rivals, are not endowed with vital significance.

Pluralistic politics requires a sense of affinity among the elites and a common attachment to the institutions and apparatus through which political life is carried on.[1] It requires some slight distance between leaders and led, not great enough to lead to a sense of utter separateness, but large enough to support self-esteem and independence of judgment.

No single party and no single social policy can be put forward as the sole embodiment of a pluralistic point of view. Democrats and Republicans, Conservatives and Labourites, Radicals, Socialists and MRP, Christian Democrats and Socialists, can all be accommodated within the confines of the political system as long as they observe the standards presented above: restriction of the political sphere and interest, gradual increments of change, the shading off and overlapping of differences, and the affinity of elites.

Only extremism is excluded. Yet many of the difficulties of the present situation come from the failure, both among conservatives and liberals, to recognize that the really crucial dividing line in politics is between pluralistic moderation and monomaniac extremism.

It has been too easy for moderates of the different positions to think that their true allies were those who appeared to espouse in a more dramatic and aggressive form their own substantive values, while their greatest enemies were those who were opposed to their substantive programs. Lib-

---

1. The strength of the forces of civility in the battle against the flood of populism was evinced in the refusal by the Select Committee of the Senate to regard Senator McCarthy's re-election in 1952 as a vindication of his actions. It said: "This is a matter for the Senate and the Senate alone. The people of Wisconsin can only pass upon issues before them. They cannot forgive an attack by a Senator upon the integrity of the Senate's processes and its committees. That is the business of the Senate."

erals and radicals have thought that revolutionaries and Communists were their allies, but were more impatient and insistent and less compromising than themselves. They believed that the revolutionaries and Communists were their allies because the extremists, too, seemed to be interested in equalitarian and humanitarian values and in the use of critical reason in social policy. The conservatives have erred in thinking that Fascists, Nazis, nativist-fundamentalists and McCarthyites were their allies because, even though their methods were distasteful, they claimed to be concerned with the protection of tradition and with the maintenance of private property. Large sections of the major parties in most Western countries have committed the mistake of believing that they have had more in common with those who claimed to represent their values by extreme and accentuated methods than they had with those who opposed them within a framework of moderation.

The mistake has been one which comes easily to mind. The entire tradition of nineteenth-century European politics accepted the continuum which ran between the extremes of left and right. It was an error which derived visual support from the seating arrangement in parliamentary chambers, but it grew out of a deeper misconception of the nature of political life.

Political standpoints and the general drifts of sentiment within parties are constellations of positions on particular issues of policy which can be schematically described as falling on a scale running between two extremes. For example, humanitarianism which entails concern for well-being, physical and psychological, ranges between a very intense degree of concern for human and even animal suffering, however slight, to that of indifference to human suffering. Similarly, liberty runs from the extreme of insistence on the right to perform, without any restraint, any conceivable action to utter indifference to liberty as a value or still further to a horror of liberty and a clear conviction as to the unqualified superiority of action prescribed by authority. Every human value can be analyzed in terms of such a scale.

Every political position, and every party platform, in its deeper implication is a complex of such values, each with its position on a scale, some high and some low.

A given position with respect to one value does not automatically entail a given position on the other scales. For example, a high degree of devotion to individual liberty does not automatically involve a given degree of devotion to humanitarianism, egalitarianism, rationalism, etc. It is one of the stereotypes inherited from the nineteenth century to believe that each constellation such as socialism, liberalism, traditionalism, is internally uniform and that liberalism, for example, is separated from conservatism by an unbridgeable gap or that socialism had nothing in common with liberalism or conservatism. Actually, there were many areas of overlapping among the parties, e.g., liberalism and conservatism both favored private property; both were more congenial to traditions of hierarchy in social status, though to different degrees, than the revolutionaries who sought complete equality; both were more congenial to a separation of the spheres than extremist romantic reaction which sought the re-establishment of hierocracy and the complete integration of society under a single ruler and a single system of values; socialism and liberalism both esteemed the power of reason and equality of opportunity, and socialism and conservatism were both anti-individualistic. Even the extremist positions were not rigorously uniform internally, as may be seen from the bitter conflicts among revolutionary sects which were, in part, at least, the product of differences interspersed among identities. Nonetheless, for reasons of tradition and because of the obvious parallels in substantive values, liberals were seen by themselves and others as having a closely sympathetic affinity with revolutionaries, while conservatives were placed very close to romantically extreme reactionaries.

This mistake has done and continues to do grievous harm in modern Western society, and the longer it persists, the more damaging it is. Both sides fail to see that a value is not enhanced by virtue of there being more of it. The establishment of a floor of status under all citizens which gives them all a minimum of dignity is not improved by rendering everyone equal in social status. Yet the latter is merely a logical extension of the former. The value of private property is not enhanced by granting unqualified license to the owners of property, nor is a certain degree of governmental regulation of monopoly less good than complete governmental control over the entire economy.

Gratification is not necessarily unilinear; furthermore, the increase in one value can jeopardize another, the passion for equality can, for example, make vain the hope of freedom, equality of status can interfere with the equality of opportunity.

The constellation of attitudes and sentiments making up a political position is poised in an equilibrium which can be easily disrupted by the extension or intensification of any of the elements. The extension to an extreme of one or two or three, such as equality or substantive justice or rationality, can very quickly break the equilibrium. This has not been sufficiently observed by either liberals or conservatives and both have, therefore, been content on the whole to count their extremist neighbors as kindred and allies.

CHAPTER 12

IDEOLOGICAL POLITICS

EXTREMISM CONSISTS in going to an extreme in zealous attachment to a particular value, e.g., private property, ethnic homogeneity, or status equality. It involves disregarding the rules which hamper the achievement of the extreme. The extremist must be deeply alienated from the complex of rules which keep the strivings for various values in restraint and balance. An extremist group is an alienated group. This means that it is fundamentally hostile to the political order. It cannot share that sense of affinity to persons or the attachment to the institutions which confine political conflicts to peaceful solutions. Its hostility is incompatible with that freedom from intense emotion which pluralistic politics needs for its prosperity. The extremity of its attachment to a given value and the passionate belief that its complete fulfillment makes all the difference in the world, is connected with its unwillingness to be satisfied with small increments. The focus of the extremist's attention on one or a few completely fulfilled values and his impatience with compromise when a plurality of values never internally consistent have to be reconciled with one another makes the extremist feel that he is worlds apart from the compromising moderates. The extremist believes in the reality and the rightfulness of disjunctions and he acts on them. This belief makes his participation in civil politics impossible, even though he has been legally elected and even though he is a member of an ordinary party.

There is an inherent mechanism in the very fact of taking an extreme position with respect to one or more values which obliterates the significance of the substantive value. Although revolutionaries and Communists say that they are interested in the equal dignity of all men, that they look forward to a regime of complete freedom and affectionate spontaneity, and that they wish to distribute power equally and to liberate the reason of man and his scientific powers so that he may rule himself in their beneficent light, the reality of their conduct is very different. Although romantic reactionaries declare they are in favor of the restoration of the primordial pieties, that they wish to conserve tradition and to maintain a regime in which inherited dignity will be accorded its proper privileges, or in which private property will be completely respected, foreign and ethnically strange elements kept suppressed and national integrity consolidated, there, too, the reality of their action is very different from their claims.

The revolutionaries, whatever they say to the contrary, do not practice the esteem of reason and science; rather they worship a rigid and ambiguous doctrine. Although they claim to be equalitarians, their own parties are steeply hierarchical and they regard the world outside those who have committed themselves to their beliefs as unutterably corrupt and unworthy. Although they say that they seek a regime of liberty and spontaneity, neither their party, nor the regime which their party establishes when it is successful, allows either of these. The revolutionary party pursues the ideal of a rigorous sect of selfless men and women, bound together by an act of belief in a sacred doctrine of extreme values. They regard the world around them as evil and as capable of cure only by violent purgation and conversion. Such a sect, even though it is called a party, can never be a party and cannot participate in civil politics.

The romantic reactionaries, aristocratic and populistic, are no different. Although they allege that they wish to conserve tradition, in practice they regard tradition as dead or corrupt or pernicious and they think that they must wipe out all that exists in order to recreate the right kind of tradition. Neither the Camelots du Roi, nor the British Union of Fascists, nor the National Socialist Party, nor the Christian Front or the most zealous populist followers of Senator McCarthy at his height found the living traditions of the society in which they lived worthy of conservation. They were convinced that they had fallen into the hands of corrupt politicians and had themselves become corrupt. It was just the living tradition of the pluralistic society which these extremists sought to destroy and which they succeeded in destroying in those countries where the tradition was weakest. Their alleged respect for the primordial pieties, for family, kinship, and soil is spurious since their extremism forces them into a position in which commitment to an ideology is the criterion of a person's or group's ultimate worth. They preach disloyalty to family and even to country and to moral obligation on behalf of an ideology which is espoused by an act of the will-to-believe. The romantic reactionary and the populistic extremist also claim to speak on behalf of the whole people and they criticize the existing pluralistic regimes for the catering to sectional and "private" interests. Although they are not infrequently subsidized by excessively worried or ideologically sympathetic rich men —businessmen and land owners—they separate themselves from their own fellow citizens and regard them as corrupt and outside the pale.

They claim to honor private property and the system of private property, but in practice they are full of hatred for the property system and for property holders. Even when property holders support them, the extremist ethic is so hostile to the element of privacy in private property that their erstwhile supporters have, on the triumph of their movement, had occasion to experience bitterly the restrictions imposed on their utilization of their property. The system of private property is too deeply rooted in civil society and it has been for many centuries too individualistic for reactionary extremists, aristocratic and populist, to find themselves truly at ease with it. They too, like the revolutionaries, find the highest form of life in segregation from the unworthy contemporary world, in a closed, tightly knit group which represents the highest ideal in all its purity. They regard the world in its present form as fit only to be cleansed by a very strong medicine.

The ideological extremists—all extremists are inevitably ideological—because of their isolation from the world, feel menaced by unknown dangers. The paranoiac tendencies which are closely associated with their apocalyptic and aggressive outlook make them think that the ordinary world, from which their devotion to the ideal cuts them off, is not normal at all; they think that it is a realm of secret machinations. What goes on in the world of pluralistic politics, in civil society, is a secret to them. It is a secret which they must unmask by vigorous publicity. Their image of the "world" as the realm of evil, against which they must defend themselves and which they must ultimately conquer, forces them to think of their enemy's knowledge as secret knowledge.

Publicity is the cure for dangerous secrecy. It is the reassurance against the hidden evil. The defensive secret, which is the companion piece of the reliance on publicity to pierce the inimical secret, is another common feature of extremism, "right" and "left." They feel that some kinds of knowledge are especially sacred. Once the enemy possesses this sacred knowledge, they are undone. It might be a password or a phrase or a ritual sentence or a doctrine or a formula, magic or scientific, but if the enemy penetrates to it, then the cause of the highest ideal is endangered. A society dominated by ideological extremism has no place for privacy, either in the conduct of the individual, in the conduct of corporate bodies, or in the relations of the various spheres or sectors of society. Privacy can too easily, as the ideological extremist sees it, be a hiding place for dangerous secrecy. The autonomy of individuals, corporate bodies and social spheres must be suspended or eliminated so that no secrets may be hidden in their folds.

CHAPTER 13

A NEW ALLIANCE

THE PLURALISTIC SOCIETY is the society of privacy and publicity. Privacy and publicity are the parallels in the focus of knowledge and sensitivity, of autonomy and co-operation based on affinity. The freedom of individuals and corporate bodies is secured in their combination.

Functional secrecy too, of course, can and must have its place in such societies. The self-protection of the society in periods of genuine external danger needs a certain amount of secrecy; so does the internal protection of the society from the conspiracy to use violence to subvert the social order. Security and counterespionage are both necessary. The need is functional; it is a practical necessity, to be assessed by sober and responsible judgment. Such secrecy is a far cry from the secrecy which is required by paranoid ideological extremism. The latter secrecy is not functional but symbolic. It is part of the war of fantasy which the pure and good conduct incessantly with corruption and evil until the Last Judgment. The secrecy demanded by ideological extremism in the United States and in Soviet Russia, in Soviet China and in the Soviet satellites is not connected with national security except by the occasion which crises provide for fanatics to focus their excited fantasies.

Just as the conservatives and liberals have been misled by their own traditions and their own thoughtlessness into believing that the similarities of substantive values were equivalent to an approximate identity of outlook between themselves and their extremist neighbors, so the similarity of the two kinds of secrets has been similarly misleading. Both policies are directed towards the preservation of secrets. One, however, is in large part and should be exclusively concerned with the functionally necessary protection of secrets, and the other is concerned with the symbolic protection of secrets which is really equivalent to maximal loyalty. The failure to distinguish has led serious persons who favor functional security to espouse symbolic or maximal loyalty-security, just as it has led some who are distressed by symbolic maximal loyalty-security to oppose functional security. The two securities have little to do with one another in fact; they resemble one another in the same way that Fascism resembles American free private enterprise or Communism resembles the British welfare state.

Partly from indolence of mind, partly from wrongheadedness and partly from misconceived self-interest, political, economic and other, an alliance was formed after the war between respectability and rowdyism, between conservatism and the lunatic fringe of the "right," between civility and extremism. In the 1930's, a complementary alliance was formed between liberalism and revolutionary extremism. Both these ill-conceived alliances should be dissolved.

The correction of the concrete loyalty-security policy which is now under way in America does not represent the end of the danger of extremism. It is rather the re-establishment of the equilibrium appropriate to our constitutional system and to the requirements of a pluralistic society. The issue is far from settled and buried forever.

In American society and in all large-scale Western societies in differing measures, the complex system of ruling values and the frictions and strains of daily life will always create a by-product of extremism in disposition and deed. Ideals are, furthermore, naturally subject to ideal interpretations and the ideological dispositions of youths and immature adults and certain types of paranoid reactions to the world guarantee that extremism can never be totally extirpated from a free society. The vitality of the tradition of extremism, revolutionary and reactionary, in all major western countries except Great Britain, makes its total elimination unlikely. It is vain to hope that extremism can ever be entirely eliminated and it is even undesirable that it should be. In a small quantity, it has the valuable function of reminding the rest of society—the pluralistic civil society with its many private interests, its compromises and its vagueness—of the ideals by which, in their most general form, it lives. There is, moreover, no chance that it can be eliminated.

Extremism does not in itself inevitably present a great danger to civil society. Russia, China, Germany and Italy, the great states which have fallen before their extremists, had neither the tradition nor institutions of a comprehensive and well-grounded pluralism. Extremism becomes a danger when it begins to set the ruling pattern, and that it can do only when it draws allies from the heart of civil society, from those whose inheritance and responsibility should bind them to a balanced pluralism. Crises like depressions and lost wars and even nominally victorious but too costly wars contribute to the process by which those most loosely moored or most unstably located become ideological extremists. Even then the danger would not be great if the great civil parties did not allow themselves to be deceived by the apparent identity of their own aims and those of their extremists. Socialist parties and liberal parties who play the Communist game, conservative parties which allow themselves to fall for the illusory protection provided by reactionary extremists, are a greater danger to pluralism than the menace of the outsiders.

The stability of the free society—of the society which acknowledges the claims of individuals and corporate bodies to privacy and which admits the proper practice of publicity based on the sense of affinity which is the matrix of autonomy —depends on the alliance of the parties at the center of the civil order.

What is called for is not a coalition government, or a "sacred alliance" which self-deceptively seeks to avoid all conflict. The alliance should involve no more than a recognition of the community of interests in the maintenance of the principle of order—an order which allows equally both conservation and change. The alliance which conservatism and liberalism must form would not involve the renunciation by either of its own traditions and its own emphases. Liberalism need not become conservative in order to discriminate itself from socialism, and socialism need not cease being socialist in order to avoid the danger of contamination by Communism. Conservatism must not turn to reaction to protect itself. Reform need not become revolution. The task equally before liberalism, conservatism and democratic socialism is to clarify their own tradition and for each to recognize what it shares with the other two.

The alliance has a common enemy. The enemy is extremism—revolutionary and reactionary. Extremism is the enemy of the autonomy of individuals and corporate bodies and of the pluralistic system of values and institutions—it is, therefore, the enemy of civil society and of the moderate politics of pluralism.

Ideological extremism is the enemy of the privacy and publicity which support our liberties. It is the progenitor of the combination of symbolic secrecy and universal publicity which is so hurtful to them.

Such an alliance will avoid the flight to the "right" and the quietism which is afflicting our educated classes today. It will lessen the tantalization of secrecy and will save the interior liberty and the sanity of American society.

BOOKS PUBLISHED BY

The Free Press

10,55